D1208906

THE ROMAN WORLD

Library Edition published 1989
Published by Marshall Cavendish Corporation
147 West Merrick Road
Freeport, Long Island
N.Y. 11520

Typeset by Jamesway Graphics
Hanson Close Middleton Manchester M24 2HD
Printed in the USA by Worzalla Publishing
Company, Wisconsin

All rights reserved. No part of this book may be
reproduced or utilized in any form or by any
means electronic or mechanical including
photocopying, recording, or by an information
storage and retrieval system, and without
permission from the copyright holder.

© Marshall Cavendish Limited
MCMLXXXVIII, MCMLXXXIX

LIBRARY OF CONGRESS
Library of Congress Cataloging-in-Publication
Data

The Roman World.
    p. cm. — (Exploring the past: 1)
    Bibliography: p.
    Includes index.
    Summary: Describes the lives and times of
Hannibal, Julius Caesar, and Cleopatra.
    ISBN 0–86307–994–6: $19.95. ISBN
0–86307–993–8 (set): $119.95
    1. Rome — History — Republic. 265-30 B.C.
— Juvenile literature. 2. Caesar, Julius —
Juvenile literature. 3. Hannibal — Juvenile
literature. 4. Cleopatra, Queen of Egypt, d. 30
B.C. — Juvenile literature. 5. Mediterranean
Region — Kings and rulers — Biography —
Juvenile literature. [1. Rome — History —
Republic, 265-30 B.C. 2. Hannibal. 3. Caesar,
Julius. 4. Cleopatra, Queen of Egypt, d. 30 B.C.
5. Generals. 6. Kings, queens, rulers, etc.] I.
Marshall Cavendish Corporation. II. Series.
DG241.2.R65 1989
937'.04 — dc 19   88–21645
                                                            CIP
                                                            AC

ISBN 0–86307–993–8 (set)
ISBN 0–86307–994–6 (vol)

The Roman World is number one in the
Exploring the Past series.

Credits: Front cover: John James;
page 1: Richard Hook; page 3: Stephen Biesty.

THE ROMAN WORLD

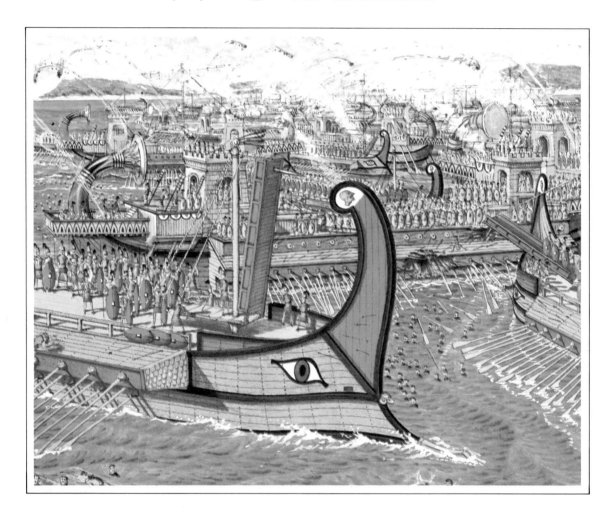

Hannibal

Julius Caesar

Cleopatra

Marshall Cavendish

NEW YORK · TORONTO · LONDON · SYDNEY

ATLANTIC CITY FREE PUBLIC LIBRAR

STAFF LIST

Series Editor
Sue Lyon

Assistant Editors
Laura Buller
Jill Wiley

Art Editor
Keith Vollans

Production Controller
Tom Helsby

Managing Editor
Alan Ross

Editorial Consultant
Maggi McCormick

Publishing Manager
Robert Paulley

Michael Holford

Titles in the EXPLORING THE PAST series

The Roman World
Hannibal
Julius Caesar
Cleopatra

The Middle Ages
William the Conqueror
Richard the Lionheart
King John

The End of Chivalry
Henry V
Joan of Arc
Richard III

The Age of Exploration
Marco Polo
Christopher Columbus
Hernán Cortés

The Italian Renaissance
Leonardo da Vinci
Michelangelo
Galileo

Shakespeare's England
Henry VIII
Elizabeth I
William Shakespeare

READER'S GUIDE

Imagine that you owned a time machine, and that you traveled back to the days when your parents were in school. Your hometown and school would look different, while the clothes, music, and magazines that your parents were enjoying might seem odd, perhaps amusing, and certainly "old fashioned" and "out of date." Travel back a few hundred years, and you would be astonished and fascinated by the strange food, homes, even language, of our ancestors.

Time machines do not yet exist, but in this book you can explore one of the most important periods of the past through the eyes of three people who made history happen. An introduction sets the scene and highlights the significant themes of the age, while the chronology lists important events and when they happened to help you to understand the background to the period. There is also a glossary to explain words that you may not understand and a list of other books that you may find useful.

The past is important to us all, for the world we know was formed by the actions of people who inhabited it before us. So, by understanding history, we can better understand the events of our own times. Perhaps that is why you will find exploring the past so exciting, rewarding and fascinating.

Peter Bull

921728

CONTENTS

Introduction ———————————————— 8

Hannibal ———————————————— 11

Portrait ———————————————— 12
Carthaginian Hero

History in the Making ———————————— 17
Crossing the Alps

The Way We Were ———————————————— 22
Carthage – Rome's Rival

Julius Caesar ———————————————— 27

Portrait ———————————————— 28
The Noblest Roman

History in the Making ———————————— 33
The Conquest of Gaul

The Way We Were ———————————————— 38
The Eternal City

Cleopatra —————————————— 43

Portrait ——————————————— 44
    Egypt's Last Queen

History in the Making ——————— 49
    Battle of Actium

The Way We Were ————————— 54
    A Scribe's Story

Appendix ——————————————— 59

Glossary ———————————————— 59

Chronology ——————————————— 60

Further Reading ————————————— 62

Index ————————————————————— 63

Top: Roger Viollet   Bottom, left to right: Scala; Michael Holford; Scala

INTRODUCTION

Richard Hook

In less than three hundred years, Rome, once a small city-state in Italy, conquered most of the known world, from Britain in the north to Mesopotamia in the east. And where Rome conquered, she stayed, to overwhelm culturally and socially as well as militarily, so that British chieftains, African merchants, and Balkan farmers all spoke Latin and thought of themselves as Roman. Ultimately, Roman citizenship, once jealously reserved to the inhabitants of the city itself, was granted to all free men; and many a man, whose ancestors had fought against the Romans, was proud to say "Civis Romanus sum" – "I am a Roman citizen."

The magic of the Roman Emperor or Caesar became so powerful that even other rulers, like Persian Shahs, or German Kaisers and Russian Czars living centuries later, borrowed the Roman title. The dream of universal empire – for the Romans spread their power over all the known civilized world excluding only untamable barbarians in the dark forest of northern Europe – again and again tempted rulers; Napoleon and Hitler both borrowed more than just the Roman eagle for their armies and new empires.

The Early Republic
The Rome that entered into the Punic Wars (the wars against Carthage that began in 264 B.C.) was not, however, very impressive. It was not particularly large – many Mediterranean cities, including Carthage, were much bigger – nor was it at all rich. Above all, it still markedly backward, and its people must have seemed uncultured to civilized Greeks. But, as the wars against Hannibal, and then against the various half-Greek monarchies of the East were to show, the Romans were tough, flexible, and able to learn from early defeats.

On its seven hills, Rome, founded five centuries earlier, controlled all Italy except the extreme north, by 270 B.C. Stamped on every coin, every public building, every military standard were the four initials SPQR – Senatus Populusque Romanus (the Senate and People of Rome) – for Rome had been a republic since its people had deposed its last king, the half-Etruscan tyrant Tarquinus Superbus, in 510 B.C. In practice, however, despite the annual gathering of the populace in the Assembly to elect the officials called

Consuls, most power was in the hands of the few aristocrats who dominated the Senate.

Roman society at this time was still very puritanical – in some ways, savagely so. Each father had complete power over even the adult members of his family; one unfortunate young man, about to make his first public speech, was dragged off the rostrum by his angry father and publicly thrashed for some misdeed. But, above all, the Romans prided themselves on their courage and refusal to panic, a quality they were to need when Hannibal, having destroyed Roman army after army, stood outside the walls. Admirably cool, the Romans raised the price of the very land on which his army was encamped!

Republican Virtues

Rome's own armies were recruited from citizens or farmers for every short war, and so were not at all professional; and, at this time, Rome had no navy whatsoever. (Carthage, by contrast, had a fleet of over 500 ships and an army of professional mercenary soldiers, while the half-Greek Seleucid empire in the East even boasted hundreds of "war elephants," raised on special elephant farms.) But Rome's army was strengthened by troops from her allies – cities that had given up their independence to Rome, but had kept their internal self-rule. Such were the small beginnings of empire.

The Romans of the 3rd century B.C. and long after idealized the small farmer, who would put on his armor to go to fight when his city called, and then, refusing honors for his victories, would return to his few acres. Cincinattus, the poor but noble Roman who had twice done just that in the 5th century B.C., was constantly cited as an example of this Roman "virtus" (a Latin word that has no precise English equivalent, but which refers to all that is best in human nature, including courage, dignity, and unselfishness). Although some nobles, even before the Republic's first overseas wars, had become large landowners, their way of life was still not so far removed from that of the common people. Going to the small Senate House through the narrow, unpretentious brick streets, nobles still wore the standard Roman dress – the toga, made of many yards of stiffly starched wool, which must have been very warm in the Italian summers. Although some Romans were already being influenced by the culture found in Greek cities like Naples or Taranto, most were still close to their peasant origins.

A Time of Change

However, when Octavian returned victorious from Egypt in 30 B.C., he returned to a very different city. Rome had grown; it was by then the largest city in the world, with over a million people packed into a small area that was still limited by its ancient walls. And it was overflowingly rich. Other Mediterranean cities had become wealthy by trading or manufacturing goods. Rome, in contrast, grew rich by conquest. In flowed tribute in the form of corn, oil, marble,

Ricciarini/Dixon

9

Aisa

silk, gold, spices – and people. For Rome's new inhabitants were, more often than not, slaves. Rome's vast conquered territories now surrounded the Mediterranean and, since it was then customary to enslave a conquered people, immense numbers had become slaves of the Romans. The Greek island of Delos, previously a lonely spot known only for its oracle who served the god Apollo, was transformed by the Romans into an immensely profitable port specializing in the slave trade and capable of handling 10,000 slaves each day.

Many of these slaves were Greeks, for Greek cities had spread across the Mediterranean, from Marseilles in southern France to Alexandria (formerly Cleopatra's luxurious capital) in Egypt. The Greeks had a far older, more sophisticated culture, which was to provide the inspiration for much of western art and thought. "Greece made captive took her conquerors captive," wrote a Roman poet, "and taught them the arts." By the time of Julius Caesar, every educated Roman spoke Greek as readily, and perhaps more elegantly, than his native Latin. Greek slaves taught the Romans not only philosophy – Brutus, leader of the Senators who murdered Caesar, was influenced by Stoicism – but also comfort and luxury. Off came the stiff, uncomfortable toga of wool; in its place, noble Romans adopted the light Greek robe, the chiton, made of cotton or even silk. Instead of the modest houses of the early Republic, Roman nobles, now immensely rich, had huge, ostentatious palaces in the heart of Rome, with baths, libraries, gardens, and banqueting halls filled with gold furniture or works of art taken from conquered cities. To run them, hundreds of slaves were needed, and armies of slaves more numerous than many a state's citizens worked the nobles' huge country estates, called latifundiae, which themselves were larger than some kingdoms.

All this grandeur was in dramatic contrast to the lives of ordinary Romans. The long wars, often fought in faraway corners of the Mediterranean, had uprooted them from their lands. When they returned after many years fighting, they might find their farms had gone to ruin or been taken over by a noble whom they were powerless to resist. Then, people had nowhere to go but the city of Rome, and little hope of making a living when they got there, since they were unable to compete with more skilled foreign craftsmen who were often slaves. Crammed into high-rise apartment buildings which frequently burned down, these "Plebeians" thronged the streets with only one thing to offer – their votes, for they were still Romans, eligible to vote in the Assembly. The great Patrician nobles bought these votes with massive bribes of games, which became ever more spectacular, with gladiators, chariots, and wild animals.

The Peace of Rome

The army, too, had changed from a body of citizens-in-arms to a highly professional corps that owed allegiance first and last to the general who paid it and led it to victory and booty. (The Republic had never found a way of paying the huge amateur armies it raised for its long wars.) This loyalty to a general rather than to the city caused endless civil wars, the last of which ended in 31 B.C. when Octavian defeated Mark Antony. From now on, Augustus – as Octavian renamed himself – decided that there would be only one triumphant general to whom soldiers would turn for pay and booty, and that wars would be fought only against external enemies. So successful was Augustus in imposing the Pax Romana, or Roman peace, that he was able to have the old walls of Rome pulled down. All new cities were now built without walls, which had never been possible before and would not happen again in continental Europe until the 19th century.

All over the empire, from Portugal to Jordan, cities sprang up or were rebuilt as "Little Romes," each complete with its own baths, aqueduct, forum, triumphal arch, and amphitheater. With only a small, distant army, the Mediterranean world entered into an age of unparalleled prosperity and luxury; the Romans, as well as spreading the benefits of efficient plumbing and good roads wherever they went, even developed central heating for the northern provinces. Above all, however, it was Rome's diffusion of Greek culture throughout Europe that civilized the barbarian north. But the Romans did not only bring peace and arts, they also introduced fair and efficient justice. First developed by magistrates in Rome, Roman law became another vital legacy of imperial rule; to this day, most law in continental Europe is based on Rome's legal system.

When the empire finally collapsed in the West – as much through civil wars as foreign invasions – Rome's former subjects did not line the roads to cheer the legions' departure. Rather, they wept over the loss of the empire and longed for its revival, still overwhelmed by the slowly decaying grandeurs of ruined temples, aqueducts, and amphitheaters.

Hannibal

With hindsight, it seems inevitable that Rome would defeat her greatest enemy, Carthage, and go on to build an empire. However, Rome's victory was by no means assured, for Carthage's navy controlled the Mediterranean Sea, and, in Hannibal, the North African city had a leader of genius. Hannibal was one of the greatest generals of the Ancient World, and he came very near to defeating Rome; but the Romans kept their nerve and eventually found in Scipio a general to equal the heroic Carthaginian leader.

HANNIBAL

One of the greatest heroes of all time, Hannibal could not conquer the mighty Romans. So why has his fame lasted for over 2,000 years?

"Daddy – please may I go with you?" Many nine-year-olds must have used these words when their fathers were off on an exciting jaunt somewhere. The young Hannibal was no exception. But the adventure he was so keen on was no ordinary day-trip – it was the conquest of what is now known as Spain.

Hannibal was a proud Carthaginian living on the North African coast where Tunisia is today. The empire of Carthage was even more ancient than that of Rome, which in the 3rd century B.C. was still rising in power and influence. Its people were the descendants of the Phoenicians, who had voyaged across the known world for centuries, reaching such farflung corners as the Canary Islands and Cornwall in search of goods in which they could trade.

Their empire had once included the Mediterranean islands of Sicily, Sardinia, and Corsica. But when Hannibal was only six, the Romans had taken these islands from Carthage, following the First Punic War. His father, Hamilcar Barca, fought in that war, and afterward, he saved Carthage itself from a revolution. As a member of a family which could trace its ancestry back to the legendary Queen Dido, founder of Carthage, Hamilcar was bitter about the loss of territory to the upstart Romans.

Hamilcar was made supreme commander of Carthage's forces, in charge of a major expedition to conquer Spain. The Romans

Personal Profile

HANNIBAL
Born *247 B.C.*   **Died** *c. 183 B.C.*
Parents *Father, Hamilcar Barca; mother unknown.*
Personal appearance *Probably had semitic features; clean shaven; fairly short and stocky; strong, with great stamina.*
General *Very courageous, he inspired great loyalty; highly intelligent, and known for his wit and wisdom. Never indulgent and allowed himself few luxuries.*

HAMILCAR (below), father of Hannibal, was a military leader who established the power of Carthage in Spain.

Mary Evans

Luisa Ricciarini

PROMISE (left) Before Hannibal and Hamilcar left their native Carthage for Spain, the boy was conducted to an altar and, "having laid his hand on the offerings . . . [swore himself] an enemy of the Roman people." Hannibal never forgot this solemn promise.

had no stake there, and the wealth of timber, minerals, and men would make up for the recent loss of Sicily. It would also make a good base for the next war against the Romans, in which his eldest son Hannibal would eventually play a major part. So, before setting out for Spain, he took Hannibal and the military commanders to a temple and made them all, including young Hannibal, swear with their hands on the sacrificial offerings on the altar that they would be enemies of Rome.

In Spain, Hannibal underwent his military training. He saw how Hamilcar, with the help of his sister's

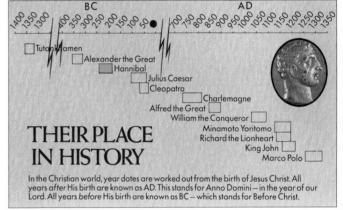

THEIR PLACE IN HISTORY

In the Christian world, year dates are worked out from the birth of Jesus Christ. All years *after* His birth are known as AD. This stands for Anno Domini – in the year of our Lord. All years *before* His birth are known as BC – which stands for Before Christ.

husband, Hasdrubal the Splendid, made treaties with Spanish cities and subdued the local tribesmen. These men would play an important role in the army Hannibal was to lead against Rome. Though Spain was officially ruled by Carthage, in practice it was Hamilcar's private kingdom. When Hamilcar was killed in battle, Hasdrubal took over, founding Cartegena, "New Carthage," on the coast. The young Hannibal was already Hasdrubal's right-hand man.

In 221 B.C., Hasdrubal was murdered by a local man. It was then that Hannibal was elected by the soldiers in Spain as their supreme leader. The authorities in Carthage did not challenge the army's choice. Even if he had not been the eldest son of Hamilcar Barca, the remarkably talented Hannibal was capable of arousing the loyalty of soldiers from many different countries.

Hannibal was well suited to leadership. For one thing, he could stay alert and healthy with very little sleep. On campaigns, he was often seen wrapped in a military cloak, cat-napping on the ground near his sentries. He could endure extremes of heat and cold, and he ate sparingly. He refused the special privileges that were

Henry Hurst

CARTHAGE In Tunis, the old harbor of Carthage (above) can still be seen.

CARTAGENA This image (right) is of Cartagena, or "New Carthage" in Spain.

Giancarlo Costa

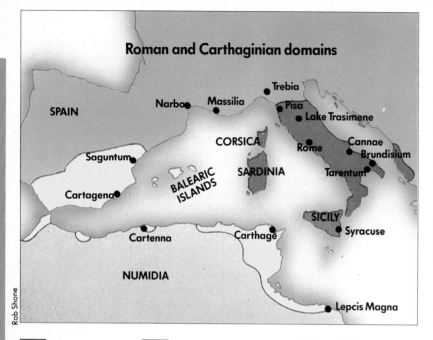

Roman and Carthaginian domains

SPAIN

Narbo • • Massilia

• Trebia
• Pisa
• Lake Trasimene

CORSICA

Saguntum •

BALEARIC ISLANDS

SARDINIA

• Rome
Cannae •
• Brundisium

Cartagena •

• Tarentum

Cartenna •

Carthage •

SICILY

• Syracuse

NUMIDIA

• Lepcis Magna

Rob Shone

■ **Romans**   ■ **Carthaginians**

traditionally due to his rank, and his men noticed that he ate what they ate and wore ordinary clothes. Most important for his popularity was Hannibal's personal courage. He always led his men into battle, and he was the last to leave the fighting.

Hannibal was a rather stern and upright character, though not without a sense of humor. The most hardworking Roman propagandists could not find a whiff of scandal to report about his private life. We only know for certain that, at about the same time as he took command of the army in Spain,

Scala

SCIPIO, the Roman Consul, was the man who finally beat Hannibal.

Hannibal married Imilce, daughter of a local chieftain, and that they had a son. Though the Romans said he was cruel, he treated his own soldiers and his allies fairly, and he took care to search for the bodies of his most distinguished opponents after battles, so that they could be given a proper burial befitting their rank.

Throughout the war, Hannibal used guile as much as force, even to protect himself. Hannibal knew that his campaign would collapse without him, and he feared an assassination attempt like that of Hasdrubal. So Hannibal had several wigs made, and different outfits to go with them. As he walked about his camp in these confusing disguises, potentially treacherous recruits could not be exactly sure what their supreme leader looked like. Hannibal was full of such tricks. On one occasion, he got out of a difficult situation by using long-horned cattle as a decoy. Blazing torches were fitted to the cattle's horns, and the Romans, who thought that Hannibal's army was trying to move away by night, were led on a wild goose chase.

The first move in the Second Punic War was Hannibal's attack on Saguntum, a city on the eastern coast of Spain, which was allied to Rome. Then, while the Romans planned retaliation in Spain, he set off to attack Italy from the direction they would

Scala

Aisa

WAR ELEPHANT In war, Carthage used African forest elephants without towers.

THE BATTLE OF ZAMA took place less than 100 miles from Carthage itself. The forces were evenly matched, but Scipio was able to stampede many of Hannibal's elephants by sounding horns as they charged. Others were channeled out of harm's way, but half of Hannibal's 40,000 men were killed.

THE BATTLE OF CANNAE

Shortly before sunrise on August 2, 216 B.C., the Roman Consul, Varro, drew up the largest army the Romans had ever fielded to face the Carthaginians on the plain below the hill of Cannae. There were about 80,000 foot soldiers and 6,000 cavalry.

Hannibal had far fewer troops—about 35,000 infantry and 10,000 cavalry—so he had planned his tactics carefully for a decisive victory with few losses. Ranged opposite the Roman infantry, Hannibal organized his infantry into a semi-circle, with the weak troops at the center, his skilled African troops on both flanks, and his cavalry on each prong of the crescent. As the Roman foot soldiers advanced, Hannibal's infantry deliberately retreated. His horsemen ran off the enemy's cavalry and positioned themselves behind the Roman lines. When Hannibal gave the signal for the infantry at the sides and the cavalry to attack the Romans were trapped. They could not escape, and the field of Cannae became a bloodbath.

The battle of Cannae lasted about eight hours, and the Roman army was all but wiped out. It was Hannibal's supreme achievement, perfect in its timing and coordination of tactics – and the worst defeat ever suffered by the Roman army. After Hannibal's stunning victory, Roman power seemed to be in peril. The defeat at Cannae had cost them both men and money. But the defeat also roused Roman resistance, and soon, the Romans were following a new strategy in Italy. Led by Generals Fabius and M. Claudius Marcellus, the army did not attempt a major battle, but instead conducted a series of skirmishes against Hannibal's men. These skirmishes continued until 211 B.C., weakening Hannibals's army and preventing the Carthaginians from gaining a secure foothold in Italy.

BATTLE POSITIONS

Mansell/Thames & Hudson/Chris Lyon

least expect – from the Alps. It was impossible that any army could cross such icy terrain, particularly a Carthaginian one, complete with their favorite terror weapon, elephants. Yet Hannibal did it. For 15 years, Hannibal held the Romans at bay in their own country. He occupied the attention of huge armies and inflicted severe defeats at Trebia, Lake Trasimene, and Cannae. It was after Trebia that, in another spectacular move, he made his army march for three continuous days and nights through the

FABIUS used small skirmishes to wear Hannibal down without a battle – "Fabian tactics."

marshes of the lower Arno.

Despite his successes, Hannibal was not able to win outright victory against the might of the Romans on their home ground. He lacked the siege equipment – mobile towers, battering rams, catapults – necessary to capture large fortified towns. Besides, despite awful casualties compared with Hannibal's, the Romans were always able to find more men, and their command of the sea kept him short of reinforcements.

Finally, after the Romans had invaded

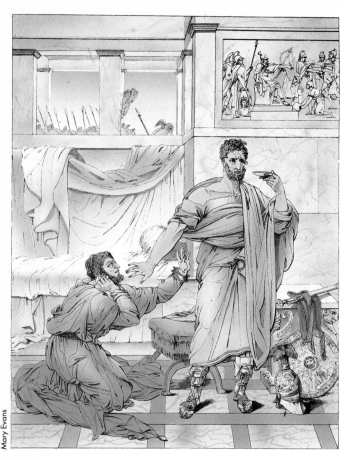

Mary Evans

Bibliotheque Nationale

PROUD DEATH (left) Hannibal chose to die by poison rather than be captured.

THE LION (right), a symbol of strength, was a part of the decoration on Hannibal's shield.

matter of time before he was caught. He was living in a secluded exile in the kingdom of Bithynia when they finally came close. He was 64 and was weary of moving on. He knew that when he was captured, the Romans would make him the centerpiece of a triumphal march, after which he would be killed anyway. So, he called for a cup of poison. His last words were: "Let us now put an end to the life which has caused the Romans so much anxiety." But his ghost remained to haunt the Romans as the only man who had seriously been able to threaten their empire.

North Africa, Hannibal had to abandon Italy in order to defend Carthage itself. The enemy now had a leader, the young and brilliant Scipio, who was a true match for Hannibal, and after the Battle of Zama, peace was declared on Roman terms. One of the conditions was the destruction of Carthage's navy. Five hundred warships were towed out to sea and set on fire.

At the age of 45, Hannibal settled in the city he had not seen since he was nine. It was no retirement, for in addition to his continuing role as Carthage's military leader, he became a "sufet," or magistrate. But his situation was uncomfortable because some of his fellow Carthaginians resented the disastrous war he had brought upon them, and his campaign against corruption made him more enemies. Scipio respected Hannibal, and these great rivals even met to talk about old times. But other important Romans, notably the senator Cato, felt that Rome would never be safe while Hannibal was alive and at liberty. In 195 B.C., when a Roman commission arrived in Carthage and his enemies were preparing to hand him over, he slipped away.

For the next 13 years, Hannibal was an illustrious exile in the courts of western Asia, giving the benefit of his experience to rulers who were still hostile to Rome. With his old guile, he just managed to keep ahead of the Roman agents following him, knowing it was only a

J.M.W. Turner/John Webb/Tate Gallery

Michael Holford

DEFEATED After Hannibal's defeat, Carthage (above) became a vassal of Rome. The city was later destroyed.

HANNIBAL on a Carthaginian coin (right) called a "triple shekel."

CROSSING THE ALPS

Elephants over the Alps? Impossible! But Hannibal managed using skill, trickery—and a vat of vinegar . . .

In the autumn of 218 B.C., Hannibal's soldiers first saw the snow-capped Alps and must have been gripped with fear at the thought of crossing them. While the local Gauls had learned to weave their way through the towering mountains, what chance had a foreign army with 60,000 men, thousands of horses, and 37 ponderous elephants? They hoped fervently that their leader would change his mind at the last minute. Instead, Hannibal urged his men forward. They had already traveled a long way, starting in Spain, passing by the Pyrenees, crossing the mighty river Rhône, and now beyond these mountains, Italy awaited them.

They were pitting themselves against more than the

Spectrum

THE ALPS
Hannibal's army confronted the immense heights of this mountain range (left) with alarm. But despite great difficulties, including the death of many of its soldiers, the army managed to cross the Alps in only 15 days.

RIVER CROSSING
The elephants, afraid of the River Rhône (left), were towed across it on rafts disguised as part of the river bank. Pont St. Esprit (below) is thought to be where they crossed.

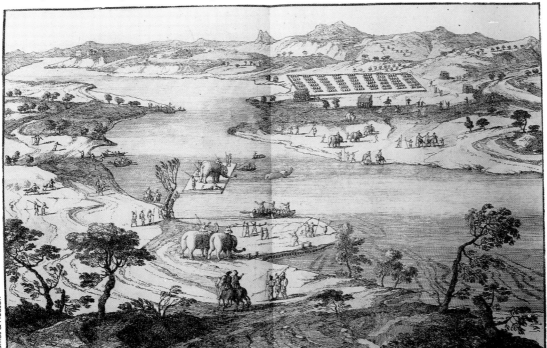

Thames & Hudson

Wolf Zeuner

natural barrier and the vicious weather – there were the local tribesmen to worry about. At first, these hostile natives were too frightened of the elephants to make a direct attack. Instead, they waited until the foreign army entered the narrow Gorge de Bourne. But Hannibal's intelligence system was always good, and when his spies told him that the tribesmen believed that war maneuvers could never take place in the darkness, he ordered all the camp fires to be lit, so that, as usual, the tribesmen went home thinking that the Carthaginians were settled for the night. Then, with great secrecy and in darkness, Hannibal left the camp with several thousand soldiers and rode ahead to take up the tribesmen's menacing ambush position. When daylight came the Carthaginians were able to charge down on the tribesmen, scattering them.

When more local tribesmen appeared offering peace, friendship, and guidance, Hannibal suspected that they planned to lead his men into another ambush. But he could not afford to ignore offers of guidance, because the Gaulish scouts already with him did not know the mountains and passes ahead. Wrong turnings were exhausting and bad for morale. He could only take the precaution of placing heavy infantry at the back of the

Rob Shone

Wolf Zeuner

Hannibal's route through the Alps

Chambéry

Vienne

Grenoble

Villard de Lars

La Mure

Valence

R. Isère

R. Drôme

R. Rhône

Montelimar

Gap

R. Arc

Bramans

Col du Mont Cenis

Lac de Savine

Col de Clapier

Susa

Turin

Col de l'Echelle

Col de Mont Genèvre

Briançon

R. Durance

Col de la Traversette

Hannibal's route

Mountain passes

Italian border

ALPINE CROSSING
Hannibal's route went via Lake Savine (below left) and Col de Clapier (center) with its very steep descent (right).

march instead of the provision-bearing animals, which he positioned right behind the cavalry. Sure enough, at the next deadly gorge, which ran along a fast-running river, possibly the river Arc, boulders came thundering into the Carthaginian train. As the wild mountain tribesmen raced like wolves after these missiles, the river went red with blood, and the mountains echoed with wild cries.

This time, the Carthaginians could do nothing but fight their way forward; and though the battle carried on through the night, they eventually beat off the attack. After this battle, the Carthaginians had to deal only with minor, sporadic attacks. Exhaustion, disease, accident, and war had greatly reduced the size of Hannibal's army. But, as they advanced into the bitterly cold inner heights of the Alps, the survivors faced the worst physical dangers.

Now, there were no more hostile tribesmen. Instead, there were piercing winds, bare rocks, and icy slopes. What remained of the general animal fodder was precious, while the thirty-seven surviving elephants,

bony under their coats made from woolen tent cloths, were barely sustained by their rations of leaves, bark, roots, and fruit. It was the tenth day of the ascent when Hannibal's men stood at the top of the pass, Col de Clapier. From there, they could see, like a mirage below them, the warm green plains of Italy. Here, they camped for two days, so that stragglers, both men and beasts, could catch up.

The sight cheered the soldiers, especially when Hannibal told them that the walls of Rome would be nothing compared with the mountainous wall they had just climbed. Nevertheless, the ordeal was far from over. The descent, which took several days, was equally arduous, as the track down was steeper than the upward one.

Suddenly, the way was blocked by a rock fall and there was no way around it. But Hannibal was undaunted and resorted to an ancient engineering strategy. Huge fires were lit on top of the rock fall, and when the roaring flames died down, the Carthaginians threw vinegar (which was really sour wine) and water onto it. This caused the rock to crumble, and when it was attacked with picks, it broke up and was cleared away. That night, the army camped in an Italian forest that offered feed to the starving horses and elephants.

Historians still debate the precise geography of each stage of the crossing of the Alps. But, out of the estimated 60,000 men who began the journey to the mountains, only about 26,000 made it to Italy. Many may have deserted. All the elephants survived the 15-day crossing, only to die in the relatively harsh Italian winter. Just one of these heroic beasts, a large Indian elephant called Surus, was still alive by the spring. Despite all their sufferings in the mountains, Hannibal and his troops men were confident. They were still in no condition to face their enemy, but they knew that they had done the impossible. That in itself was a great victory.

HANNIBAL'S FORCES

NUMIDIANS made the best light cavalry. They rode bareback and wore no armor.

CARTHAGINIAN cavalry were nobles, while citizens made up the infantry.

SPANISH cavalry often fought on foot. Their headgear was made of sinew.

Peter Bull

CARTHAGE-ROME'S RIVAL

If Hannibal had conquered the Romans, we might now be writing in Punic script rather than Roman letters.

The two greatest powers in the Mediterranean world in the third and second centuries B.C. were Rome and Carthage. Their deadly rivalry came to a head with the Punic Wars, when Carthage produced excellent military leaders, such as Hamilcar Barca and his son Hannibal.

But the might of Rome toppled Carthage, and the remains of Hannibal's city now lie buried under the ruins of a Roman city, built a century later where Carthage had stood.

According to legend, Carthage, meaning "new town,"

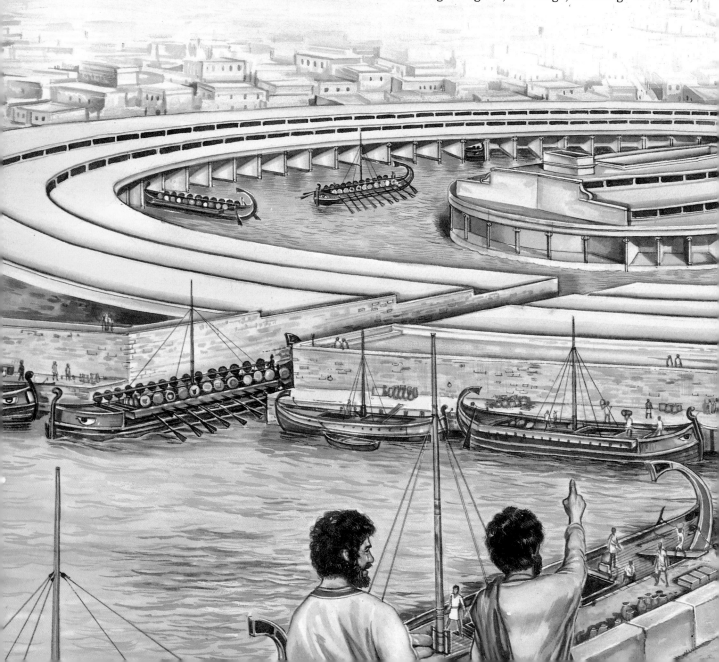

was founded by Dido, the exiled sister of the King of Tyre (Lebanon) and a band of fellow Phoenicians. Dido bought land on the peninsula beside the bay of Tunis from a local chief, Iarbus. In the language of legends, she asked for as much land as could be obtained by an oxskin, and outwitted Iarbus by cutting a hide into little strips and claiming what they surrounded. When Carthage prospered, Iarbus threatened war unless Dido became his wife. She defied him by throwing herself on a huge funeral pyre.

In Hannibal's day, nearly six centuries later, a sacred grove dedicated to Dido remained in the city. By then, Carthage was the center of a commercial spider's web, which stretched east to Egypt, west to Spain, and as far as the Canary Islands, the Cameroons, and even the Azores. Its warehouses were full of gold and silver, lead and tin, pitch and esparto grass, the skins of deer, lions

Peter Bull

FLASH BACK

LIFE IN CARTHAGE

BAAL (left) was the chief god in Carthage, but the goddess Tanit was more popular. She demanded cruel sacrifices: in the burial chamber (above) the cremated remains of sacrificed children were found.

GOLD (above) was imported from Senegal and was used in jewelry worn by both men and women in Carthage. The designs were often poor copies of Greek work. The glass amulet and vase (below) were made by Phoenician craftsmen.

TANIT (right) was a goddess of fertility, and her power was immense. The Romans saw her as savage because the Carthaginians made terrible human sacrifices to please her. Her symbol (inset) has been found in Punic ruins all over North Africa.

A RAZOR in bronze (top) is marked in imitation of Egyptian art. The Carthaginians were traders more than they were artists and often copied the work of other cultures. The terracotta jar (above) may have been used to store olive oil.

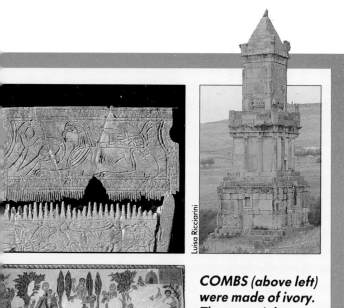

Luisa Ricciarini

C.M. Dixon

COMBS (above left) were made of ivory. The tower (above right) is a Punic mausoleum in Tunisia. The Roman mosaic (left) depicts scenes from life on an estate near Carthage.

C.M. Dixon

wealth from trade, the sea teemed with fish, and the land behind Carthage was fertile. In summer, when the city was uncomfortably hot and dry, the wealthy merchants could leave their palaces and retire to pleasant country estates.

Carthage was always noisy and crowded. Because there was so little space, the houses of ordinary people were often on an upper floor with shops on the ground level. Some buildings are said to have risen to seven stories. In many respects, Carthage was not unlike a North African town today.

When a Roman thought of a Carthaginian, he automatically thought of a merchant. In one Roman play, the hero is a Carthaginian dealer in small goods. His cargo includes shoe straps, pipes, nuts, and panthers, a list that was meant to raise a laugh at the Punic way of making money out of everything under the sun.

There is no doubt that the Carthaginians were practical wheeler-dealers rather than dreamy artists, but they were not uncultured. The merchants who did business in so many markets often spoke several languages, especially Greek and Latin. At home, they had their own alphabet, and, when the Romans destroyed Carthage, they also destroyed libraries full of books in Punic, which was related to Hebrew. But significantly, the only Carthaginian works we know about are practical: Mago's handbook on agriculture and Hanno's account of his voyage to West Africa.

The Carthaginians' rivals, first the Greeks and later the Romans, respected their form of government, which was relatively democratic. From among the merchant princes, two "sufets," or judges, were elected. These men had the power to summon the city's council, which met in the open and was composed of leading merchants who had been elected by every free man.

In addition to the sufets, Carthage had a state treasurer, a censor of public morals, and individual officials who were responsible for the upkeep of the harbor, the street markets, and public buildings. The sufets had no military power, and, in case they might try to make themselves into kings, military men had no political power. Generals were frequently reminded that they were the servants of the people, and when they were defeated in battle, they could expect punishment. There are records of failed Carthaginian generals who were exiled or even crucified.

In addition to being famous for its handling of money and its politics, Carthage was known for its severe religion, which sometimes involved the ritual burning of young children. Their supreme male god, Baal, was

and leopards, as well as elephant tusks – the African ivory trade was one Carthaginian monopoly – and precious perfumes. These busy people specialized in making objects from imported raw materials, objects which they could then export, although they also traded in goods made by others. The Romans, for example, regarded Punic mattresses as luxuries, and more backward peoples prized Punic cloth. The word "Punic" refers to the Carthaginians.

Thanks to her navy, Carthage was queen of the sea. She had trading agreements with all the peoples of the Mediterranean, and her warships dealt sternly with pirates. Not surprisingly, the city of Carthage was dominated by a massive double harbor. The outer harbor, which could be barred to the open sea by iron chains, was reserved for trading ships. The inner harbor was the navy's headquarters, shaped like a wheel, the berths for 200 galleys forming the spokes for the artificial island that was the hub.

This island was topped by a signal tower, from which the outer water could be watched. It was all enclosed by a wall, so that unauthorized people could not observe day-to-day activities within the top-secret harbor.

The hilly city focused on this harbor and its surrounding outbuildings, sheds, and quays. In addition to the

FLASH BACK

Trade and Agriculture

Hutchinson

LEPTIS MAGNA (left) was a trading port colonized by Carthage. The ivory furniture panel (right) illustrates three things exported by Carthage – slaves, wild beasts, and ivory objects, all prized by the rich.

Michael Holford

DYED WOOL in a Tunisian market (right) is a reminder that Carthage was famous for its dyes.

FRUIT, such as pomegranates (below left) and figs (below right), were grown around Carthage.

Spectrum

OLIVE TREES (left) were grown mainly to produce olive oil for export.
Ardea

FARMING Carthaginians were mainly merchants, but some of them owned land outside the town where they grew fruit and reared sheep (right), all commodities for trading.

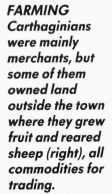

Hutchinson

regarded as the creator of the universe. Hannibal, which was a common Carthaginian name, means "Favored by Baal," while Hasdrubal means "Helped by Baal." To continue protecting his worshipers and fertilizing the earth, Baal demanded human and animal blood. At Carthage, worship was focused on Baal's consort Tanit, a mother goddess who brought fertility to the world.

After Hannibal's defeat, the peace between Rome and Carthage lasted more than 50 years. Then Numidia, Rome's ally, began to expand at Carthage's expense. The Third Punic War began in 149 B.C., when Carthage retaliated. The Romans besieged Carthage and captured it in 146. The last defenders set fire to the temple where they had taken refuge and burned in the flames.

For ten days or more, fires raged in the city. Keeping all the precious objects for the State, the Roman commander, Scipio, grandson of Scipio Africanus who defeated Hannibal, allowed his men to plunder. All Carthaginians who surrendered were sold into slavery, and every building left standing was obliterated. A curse was pronounced on the charred ground, and after a plow had been ritually drawn over it, salt was sown in the furrow. As far as the Roman Republic was concerned, Carthage would remain barren and uninhabited forever.

Julius Caesar

ulius Caesar has been described as devious, ruthless, and financially corrupt. At the same time, he was a brave soldier, a gifted writer, and an efficient ruler of his city. There were many contradictions in his character, but his achievements in peace and war are undoubted. Even his assumption of dictatorial power seems to have been popular with most Romans. Caesar refused the monarchy, but after his murder, his nephew Octavian (renamed Augustus) soon became Rome's first Emperor.

Tony Masero

JULIUS CAESAR

A brilliant politician and general, Caesar achieved much for the glory of Rome and her people.

Personal Profile

JULIUS CAESAR

Born *July 12, 100 B.C., Rome.*
Died *March 15, 44 B.C., Rome.*
Parents *Caius Julius Caesar and Aurelia.*
Marriage *Cornelia 84 B.C., Pompeia 67 B.C., Calpurnia 59 B.C.*
Children *Julia 82 B.C. (with Cornelia), possibly Caesarion 47 B.C. (with Cleopatra).*
Personal appearance *Tall and well-built, with dark eyes and fair hair. Caesar wore his thinning hair short and was always clean shaven and immaculately dressed.*
General *Caesar was highly intelligent, and ambitious enough to use bribery, murder, or generosity to achieve his ends. He had a mild form of epilepsy, which caused blackouts.*

The sun shone on the huge crowd in the Forum. It was February 15, 44 B.C.—the day of the Lupercalian Festival, one of the most important religious events in ancient Rome. Julius Caesar was making a speech on the *rostra*, when suddenly he was offered a crown. Caesar reached out to accept the symbol of kingship . . . and hesitated. He was already the most powerful man in Rome; he held the offices of Consul and Dictator for life. But he also had enemies in the Senate who feared his power.

Caesar glanced around the crowd—were they ready to accept a king again? "Jupiter alone is King of the Romans," Caesar declared, and had the crown sent to the temple of Jupiter. The crowd cheered their approval. Caesar had judged their mood well. It was typical of him—he was a shrewd politician who always knew which actions would be popular.

Caesar's strength of character developed at an early age. He was born into an impoverished branch of a noble family. As a boy, he was an able scholar and soon developed a love for Greek culture. He was also a good sportsman, skilled in athletics, fencing, and riding. By the age of 15, he had married and found an interest in politics. Caesar spent time in the army—on the staff of Marcus Thermus, the governor of Asia—and on his return to Rome, practiced law for a time. He then

CAPTURED BY PIRATES *On his way to study under the Greek master Apollonius Molon in Rhodes in 76 B.C., Caesar was captured and held for ransom. On his release, he boldly swore to return and crucify the pirates, which he did with speed and efficiency!*

Giancarlo Costa

journeyed to the Greek island of Rhodes to study public speaking under Apollonius Molon.

Caesar soon became heavily involved in politics, and in 65 B.C. was made Curule Aedile—the officer in charge of public entertainments. Determined to make himself popular, Caesar spent vast amounts of money providing the people of Rome with enjoyable events. He organized gladiatorial games and festivals on a scale Rome had never seen before.

At the same time, Caesar delivered impressive speeches and acquired some very influential friends. Among them were two of the most powerful men in Rome—Marcus Licinius Crassus, an immensely rich

"I AM NOT KING . . ." *Caesar refused the symbol of kingship (above), but some still feared he would revive the title.*

ANCIENT RUINS (below) *All that remains today of the Roman Forum, once the center of daily life in ancient Rome.*

Scala

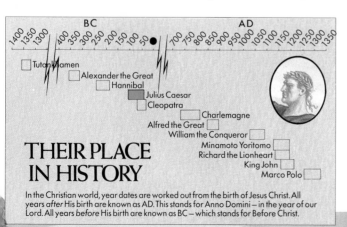

THEIR PLACE IN HISTORY

BC		AD

Tutankhamen
Alexander the Great
Hannibal
Julius Caesar
Cleopatra
Charlemagne
Alfred the Great
William the Conqueror
Minamoto Yoritomo
Richard the Lionheart
King John
Marco Polo

In the Christian world, year dates are worked out from the birth of Jesus Christ. All years *after* His birth are known as AD. This stands for Anno Domini – in the year of our Lord. All years *before* His birth are known as BC – which stands for Before Christ.

Giancarlo Costa

INSPIRED BY ENVY
In 70 B.C., Caesar took up an appointment in Spain, but found his life there boring. Then, in Cadiz, he saw a statue of Alexander the Great and felt envious that Alexander had conquered the world before he was 33. Caesar was inspired by this thought and went on to conquer vast new territories himself.

man who loaned Caesar the huge sums of money he spent as Curule Aedile, and Gnaeus Pompeius (Pompey), a very successful and popular general.

The conquest of more and more new territories brought enormous wealth into Rome, but corruption and political violence became common, and efficient government was impossible.

Against this background, in 60 B.C., Caesar persuaded Crassus and Pompey to join him in a bid to gain control of the Senate. By bribing voters, Caesar would be selected Consul—the most important office in Rome—and would then enact laws favorable to Crassus and Pompey. The "triumvirate" made a powerful team—Caesar provided the ambition, Crassus the wealth, and Pompey the military power.

Much of what they did was not entirely honest. But Caesar achieved his aims and gained more power. He made himself Governor of the Roman provinces of Cisalpine and Transalpine Gaul, and had command of

CICERO DEMANDS THE DEATH PENALTY

In 63 B.C. Marcus Tullius Cicero was elected Consul, and prevented a rebellion against the State by the man he defeated, Lucius Sergius Catilina. In the Senate, Cicero demanded the death sentence for Catilina. Caesar called for imprisonment only. Cicero—the only man who could better Caesar at persuasive speaking—won!
Cicero, six years older than Caesar, was a brilliant lawyer and speech-maker. He sided with Pompey in the civil war, but was later reconciled with Caesar.

CROSSING THE RUBICON
January 10, 49 B.C.

Julius Caesar, standing on the northern bank of the River Rubicon, faced the most critical decision of his career. "We may still draw back," he told his companions, "but, once across that little bridge we shall have to fight it out."

The Rubicon marked a political boundary between Gaul and Italy. Worried about Caesar's increasing power and popularity, the Senate had ordered Caesar to resign as Governor of Gaul, and disband his troops and return to Rome. But Caesar knew that if he did return without his army, he would be defenseless against his enemies in the Senate. Yet, if he took his men across the river, he would be committing an act of treason against Rome. This he knew would lead to civil war. As he pondered his decision, legend has it that a vision of superhuman size appeared by the river, playing a reed pipe. Some of Caesar's men heard the music, too, and moved toward the bank to watch. Suddenly, the ghostly figure snatched a trumpet from one of the men and, giving a long, loud blast on the horn, drifted across the river.

"Let us accept this as a sign from the gods," Caesar cried out, "and follow where they beckon, in vengeance on our double-dealing enemies." And Caesar led his army across the Rubicon, and into civil war.

The rivalry between Caesar and Pompey had come to a head. Caesar proved his might quickly, and within 60 days, he had driven Pompey's army out of Italy. Caesar's pursuit was relentless. After crushing Pompey's forces in Spain, he followed them across the Adriatic Sea to Pharsalus, in Greece; and in 48 B.C., Caesar won a decisive battle there against Pompey. Pompey fled to Egypt, where he was treacherously murdered in 47 B.C.

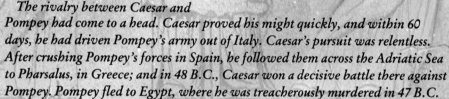

The heavy broken line marks the boundary between Gaul and Italy.

large armies there. Between 58 and 50 B.C., Caesar used this army to conquer vast new territories in other parts of Gaul and also raided southern Britain. These successes bolstered his popularity at home and won him the devotion of his soldiers.

In 53 B.C., Crassus was killed in battle, and Caesar and Pompey became increasingly bitter rivals. While Caesar was amassing vast wealth with his conquests in Gaul, Pompey was establishing himself as the champion of the government in Rome. The rivalry between the two great men came to a head in 49 B.C.—and landed Rome with a

CALPURNIA dreamed of Caesar's murder.

civil war. In a lightning campaign the following year, Caesar defeated Pompey in Greece.

Pompey fled to Egypt and was promptly put to death by the Egyptian king, Ptolemy XIII. Despite being rivals, Caesar avenged Pompey's death by defeating the Egyptian king, and placing the government of Egypt in the hands of Ptolemy's sister, Cleopatra. And for once in his life, Caesar allowed his emotions to interfere with his politics. While he flirted and cruised up the Nile with Cleopatra, his enemies were gathering their forces. But to no avail!

Before returning to Rome, Caesar won a crushing victory over Pharnaces, the son of Mithridates, in Pontus (northern Asia Minor). So swift was his defeat of the unfortunate Pontic leader that Caesar was inspired to make his memorable statement: "Veni, Vidi, Vici," — "I came, I saw, I conquered." Then in North Africa, he was victorious over King Juba of Numidia (Algeria). And with his great triumphs behind him — Gaul, Alexandria, Pontus, Africa, and Spain — Caesar entered Rome in 47 B.C. to a jubilant welcome. One whole month was spent in celebration. Only a few days separated each of four magnificent triumphal processions.

By 45 B.C., Caesar's power in Rome was almost absolute. Now, he set about dealing with the political and social problems that had built up in the city over the years. He opened the Senate to men who were not nobles, launched many new building projects, passed new laws, and updated methods of collecting taxes.

His far-reaching reforms brought benefits to the lower classes, but made Caesar very unpopular with the nobles. Many already felt that Caesar had become too powerful. And, since the incident with the crown at the Festival of the Lupercalia in February, many were convinced that Caesar would become king. On March 15, 44 B.C., a group of senators put an end to Caesar's ambitions. They stabbed him to death, then declared that republican freedom was restored to Rome. But all they did was plunge Rome into another civil war, between themselves and the friends of Caesar.

British Museum

THE IDES OF MARCH
On March 15, 44 B.C., Caesar went to the Senate to be greeted by drawn daggers. He died with 23 wounds on his body. A coin (both sides shown left) was struck to mark his death.

A SENSELESS DEED
Caesar (right, in the uniform of a general) was murdered to prevent another monarchy. But Caesar's adopted son, Octavian, became, as Augustus, virtual Emperor of Rome in 30 B.C.

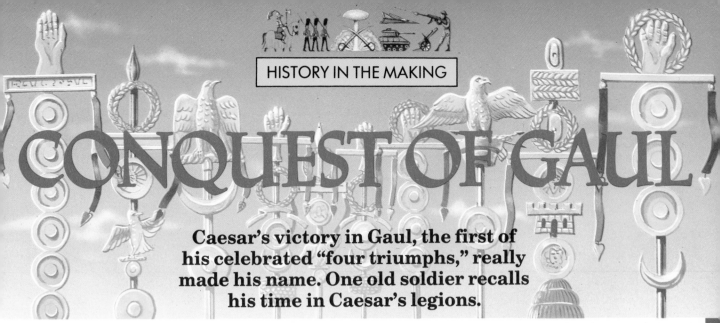

CONQUEST OF GAUL

Caesar's victory in Gaul, the first of his celebrated "four triumphs," really made his name. One old soldier recalls his time in Caesar's legions.

I was a legionary when Caesar came to take command in Gaul. None of us knew much about him then, though one man had fought under Caesar in Spain and said that he was a good general.

When he arrived in Gaul, Caesar told us how proud he was to be commanding us. Then the training started! Caesar demanded perfection in all types of drill—from throwing the spear *(pilum)* and using the short sword *(gladius)* to camp building and formation marching. Of course, this was hard work, but we admired him for being so careful about training. After all, it was for our own benefit!

Our first chance to put our training into practice was when those wild barbarians, the Helvetii, invaded from the mountains. Caesar led us forward at once. Unlike some generals who skulk at the back of a fight, Caesar

Giancarlo Costa

FINAL SURRENDER
Vercingetorix lays down his arms at Caesar's feet (left). Six years later, he was exhibited in Caesar's triumphal procession in Rome. Vercingetorix was then executed!

CAESAR'S ROME
The Roman empire before and after Caesar's conquests.

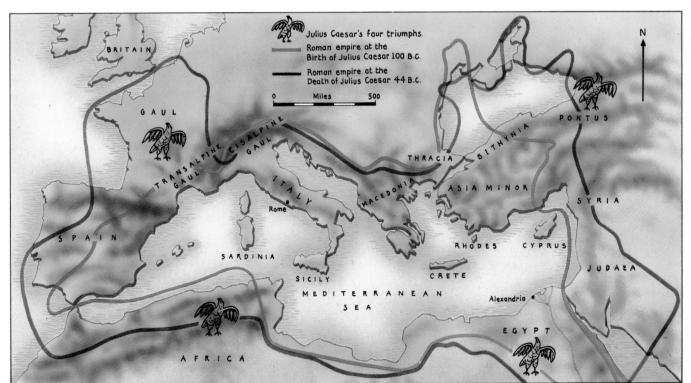

Julius Caesar's four triumphs.
Roman empire at the Birth of Julius Caesar 100 B.C.
Roman empire at the Death of Julius Caesar 44 B.C.

0   Miles   500

N

BRITAIN

GAUL

TRANSALPINE GAUL

CISALPINE GAUL

ITALY

Rome

SPAIN

SARDINIA

SICILY

MEDITERRANEAN SEA

AFRICA

MACEDONIA

THRACIA

BITHYNIA

PONTUS

ASIA MINOR

SYRIA

RHODES   CYPRUS

CRETE

JUDAEA

Alexandria

EGYPT

Andrew Farmer

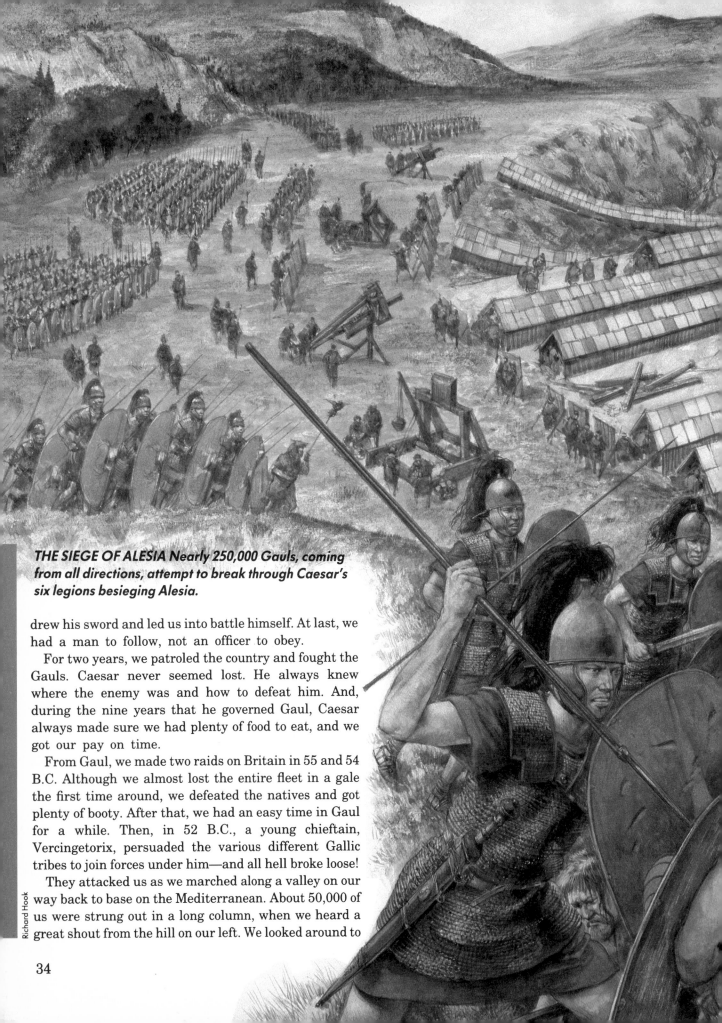

THE SIEGE OF ALESIA *Nearly 250,000 Gauls, coming from all directions, attempt to break through Caesar's six legions besieging Alesia.*

drew his sword and led us into battle himself. At last, we had a man to follow, not an officer to obey.

For two years, we patroled the country and fought the Gauls. Caesar never seemed lost. He always knew where the enemy was and how to defeat him. And, during the nine years that he governed Gaul, Caesar always made sure we had plenty of food to eat, and we got our pay on time.

From Gaul, we made two raids on Britain in 55 and 54 B.C. Although we almost lost the entire fleet in a gale the first time around, we defeated the natives and got plenty of booty. After that, we had an easy time in Gaul for a while. Then, in 52 B.C., a young chieftain, Vercingetorix, persuaded the various different Gallic tribes to join forces under him—and all hell broke loose!

They attacked us as we marched along a valley on our way back to base on the Mediterranean. About 50,000 of us were strung out in a long column, when we heard a great shout from the hill on our left. We looked around to

Richard Hook

see hundreds of horsemen pouring over the crest of the hill. Dressed in long, flowing capes of bright colors and checked trousers, the Gauls looked truly ferocious. They came galloping down toward us, waving their swords and screaming war cries.

Our centurion ordered us to left-turn and close shields. As we did so, the Gauls smashed into the men guarding our baggage wagons like a thunderbolt. Using their spears and long swords, the Gauls killed many men and made off with several wagons. Our solid line of shields and short spears held the Gauls at bay until our own cavalry came and drove them away.

We buried the dead and then started after the attackers. We followed their trail to the large hillfort of Alesia. Unlike other hillforts that we had attacked, this one had strong stone walls and impressive towers. At once, Caesar ordered us to dig trenches and build walls right around Alesia. Caesar planned to starve the Gauls of fresh supplies and force Vercingetorix into surrendering. We worked for days, and even doubled our efforts when Caesar learned from his spies that the Gauls were raising a fresh army.

A LEGIONARY had a heavy load! His helmet weighed 6lbs, mail shirt 22lbs, shield (wood and leather) 25lbs, and equipment totaled 40–60lbs. This included a spade (1), pickax (2) and mattock (3) for trench-digging, a wooden stake (4) for defensive fencing, food, cooking pots (5,6), and personal satchel (7). He also had a light and heavy spear (8,9), sword (10), and a cloak that doubled as a blanket.

Richard Hook

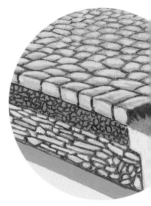

ROMAN ROADS
The army built roads as they marched. Roads had drainage ditches, and up to four levels: sand, stone slabs in cement, crushed stone in cement, and stone block surface.

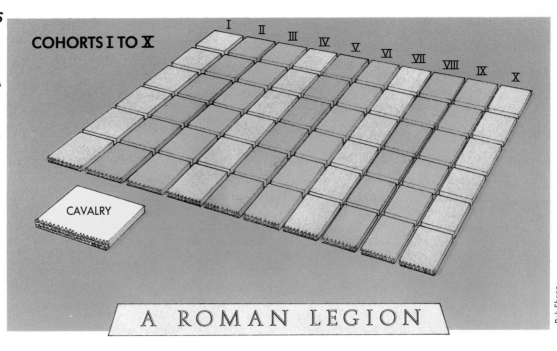

CAESAR'S LEGIONS
Each legion—about 3,600 men—was made up of 10 cohorts. Each cohort had six centuries of 60 men, plus a centurion (leader), a signifer (standard bearer), an optio (rearguard officer), and a cornicen (hornblower) or tubicen (trumpeter). Roman cavalry was weak, but Caesar used foreign horsemen in battle.

COHORTS I TO X

CAVALRY

I II III IV V VI VII VIII IX X

A ROMAN LEGION

Rob Shone

MILITARY BRIDGE
To enable his army to cross the mighty river Rhine, Caesar built a bridge in just 10 days. It was about 4 yards wide, on 50 supports 7½–8½ yards apart. He destroyed the bridge 18 days later.

Then, early one morning, we got the order to arm ourselves for battle. We were drawn up facing the west. About noon, a huge army of Gauls came into sight. There were thousands of them. They filled the entire valley—three miles wide from hilltop to hilltop—with their gaily colored clothes and flashing armor.

Their cavalry advanced and were thrown back. Then, the Gauls rushed at us screaming and yelling, as their arrows and sling-stones rained down upon us. We threw our spears, then drew our swords. We met the Gauls with a mighty crash, and everyone was shouting at once. The Gauls were tough fighters, and their long swords were vicious weapons, but they had no training for close fighting. We jabbed at them with our short swords, and protected each other with our line of shields. The Gauls fought independently—and got the worst of it.

It was a hard battle, and lasted for several hours. As dusk fell, the Gauls fled to a nearby hill. After several attempts to break through our lines, the Gallic army pulled back, and Vercingetorix was forced to surrender Alesia. It was a great victory for us and for Caesar.

The capture of Alesia ensured Caesar's reputation as a great general and made him a Roman hero. With the conquest of Gaul, his power in Rome increased. And Gaul itself was changed dramatically and forever by Alesia. Instead of being a collection of small, warring kingdoms, Gaul became unified under Roman control and enjoyed the benefits of Mediterranean civilization.

I came back to Gaul when I retired from the army, just after the celebrations in Rome for Caesar's four "triumphs." Oh yes, I enjoyed my time in the legions, but farming is about as much excitement as I want now!

THE ETERNAL CITY

From humble beginnings, Rome became the center of the most powerful empire in the world.

Rome began as a small group of farming villages between seven hills beside the river Tiber. About 800 B.C., these villages became united under a king. According to Roman legend, the first king was Romulus. He and his twin brother, Remus, founded the city in 753 B.C., on the spot where their lives had been saved. As babies, the boys had been left in the open to die, but were found and cared for by a she-wolf.

THE ROMAN FORUM looking toward Capitoline Hill. Buildings were made of stone and concrete with terracotta roof tiles. Many buildings bore the initials SPQR—Senatus Populusque Romanus (The Senate and the People of Rome). Key: 1 Forum of Caesar 2 Temple of Romulus 3 Temple of Caesar 4 Basilica Julia (a meeting place) 5 the Rostra 6 Curia (or Senate House) 7 Tabularium (Public Records Office) 8 Temple of Jupiter.

FLASH BACK

CITY LIFE

The theater was an important part of Roman entertainment. Pantomime (above) was very popular. Masked actors mimed or danced a story and had their fans, just as actors do today.

Glass was used to make simple containers for practical use (below) and also for more decorative pieces (below left).

A Roman water heater (above). Liquid was heated as it passed from the cylinder through the wall around the fire box.

The city grew under successive kings until, in 510 B.C., Tarquinus Superbus—the seventh king—proved to be such a bad ruler that the people rose against him. Instead of putting their trust in another king, the Romans decided to govern themselves, with two Consuls in charge who would have to be elected each year. This form of government—a republic—governed Rome until the time of Caesar.

During the early days of the Republic, the citizens of Rome were divided into two classes. They were Patricians—noblemen who held the top appointments and the only ones who could become members of the Senate, the body which ruled Rome; and Plebeians—ordinary people such as farmers, tradesmen and artisans. In the early days of the Republic, the Plebeians were completely excluded from power. They were so opposed to this idea that they threatened to set up a separate city. To prevent this from happening, they were given their own special officials called Tribunes. These officials had extensive powers: they had the power of veto over the Senate and other Patrician officials and were guaranteed immunity from harm.

With wars and conquests, the Republic prospered and grew, and, at the same time, its social and political structures evolved. After the wars with Hannibal in 219-202 B.C., many of the Plebeians lost their farms and went to Rome, swelling the city's population dramatically. To survive, many of these became "clients" or

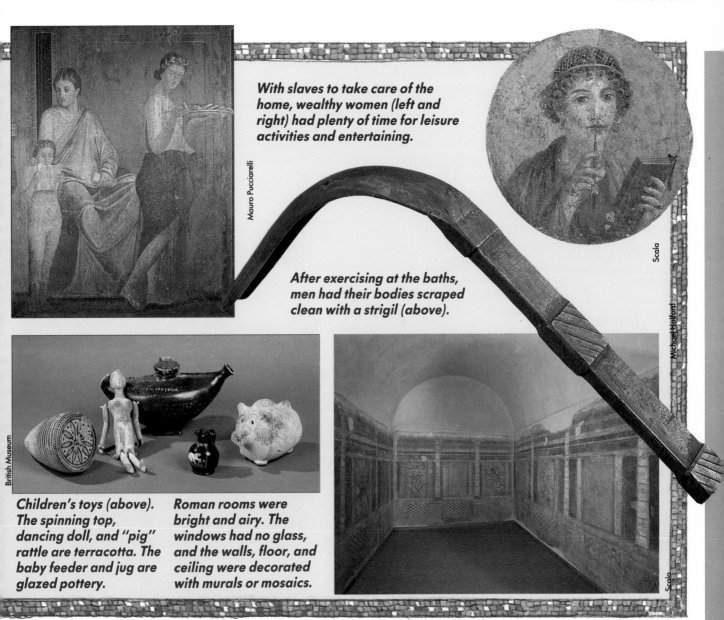

With slaves to take care of the home, wealthy women (left and right) had plenty of time for leisure activities and entertaining.

After exercising at the baths, men had their bodies scraped clean with a strigil (above).

Children's toys (above). The spinning top, dancing doll, and "pig" rattle are terracotta. The baby feeder and jug are glazed pottery.

Roman rooms were bright and airy. The windows had no glass, and the walls, floor, and ceiling were decorated with murals or mosaics.

hangers-on of the Patricians. This meant that each Patrician could use his Plebeian clients to vote on his behalf in elections. Effectively, this meant that Rome's government was controlled by a few very rich people.

On the whole, life in Rome was civilized. Most people lived in apartments, often seven or more stories high. The streets in between were often narrow—barely wide enough for a cart to pass through—but many streets had fountains of fresh drinking water. Although streets were often littered with mud and horse droppings, well-placed stepping stones allowed people to cross in safety.

Romans bought their food and other goods from the numerous shops and markets in the city. Home cooking was rare, and most people ate in cafés or bought food from vendors in the street. The poor existed on a diet of bread, porridge, and scraps of meat. Only rich business-men and Patricians indulged in huge feasts prepared in their kitchens by slaves. At banquets, dishes such as roast ostrich, oysters, dormice, baked hams, and stuffed dates were served in huge quantities.

Roman traders had workshops near their homes and employed a few dozen people. They produced large quantities of goods such as pottery, leatherwork, iron pots, military equipment, and furniture. There were no large factories; and everything was made by hand.

When they were not working, most Roman men enjoyed visiting the baths, large, luxurious buildings where men not only washed themselves, but also exercised, met their friends, and arranged business deals. Women did not visit these establishments—they had their own private baths—but they did accompany the men to the theater and the races. Chariot racing was extremely popular, and large sums of money were bet on the outcome of each race.

On special holidays, more exciting spectacles were organized. The most dramatic were the Games, which took place in large arenas where thousands of people could watch. Gladiator fights were the most popular event, where men—usually criminals, slaves or captives—were forced to fight each other to the death. If a gladiator had fought particularly well, he could appeal to the crowd for mercy. If they waved their handker- chiefs, the man would be spared. If they pointed their thumbs down, the man was killed. Sometimes, for greater excitement, gladiators would be blindfolded or pitched against wild animals. Although the odds were against them, some gladiators did survive and even earned their freedom by fighting well.

In later years, the Games became increasingly spectacular. Sometimes an arena was flooded, and the gladiators fought from ships. But the Games were perhaps the most unsavory aspect of Roman culture.

FLASH BACK

THE GAMES

Bronze gladiator's helmet (above). A gladiator did not often survive against wild animals (left).

Scala

Chariot races were fast and furious. Charioteers could earn vast sums of money, but could also be thrown or dragged to their deaths.

Giancarlo Costa

Up to 300 pairs of gladiators fought in each show in Caesar's time. Samnites (2) and Mirmillones (3) were armed with short sword and shield. Thracians (4) had a curved dagger and small shield. The Retiarius (1) had only a net and trident. Gladiator fights were banned in A.D. 325, but went on for another two centuries.

Francis Phillips

SER PENIIVS

Cleopatra

he Romans, who blamed her for the civil wars between Mark Antony and Octavian, belittled Cleopatra as an oriental temptress who had used womanly wiles to lead Antony astray from his duties to Rome. Her popular reputation is still based on this view, but Cleopatra was a far more complex and interesting character – a civilized, cultured and clever politician whose aim was to keep Egypt independent of Rome. Perhaps her failure was inevitable, for, by the 1st century B.C., Rome was well on the way to universal empire.

Nick Harris

Cleopatra—a brilliant queen, beloved by her people—enticed the two most important men in Rome.

"Break open the door!" yelled the Roman centurion, gazing angrily at the barred entrance to the great tomb Cleopatra had built for herself in Alexandria. Immediately, burly soldiers began pounding away with a makeshift battering ram, and in less than a minute, they had burst the doors apart and were running inside.

But it was too late. There on a golden couch stretched the lifeless body of Cleopatra. Nearby on the cold marble floor lay her maid Iras, also dead. As the centurion moved closer, he saw two tiny pinpricks on the bare skin of Cleopatra's left arm and a deadly asp slithering away . . .

The Roman Consul Octavian cursed when he heard the news. So Cleopatra had denied him the glory of parading her in triumph through the streets of Rome after all. Well, now they were both dead: Cleopatra and Mark Antony, her Roman lover, who had killed himself a few days earlier. Perhaps Octavian reflected on the sad story of Cleopatra's life.

She was born in 69 B.C., daughter of Ptolemy XII Auletes, one of the Greek kings who had ruled Egypt ever since the time of Alexander the Great. Throughout

Personal Profile

CLEOPATRA VII
Born *69 B.C.*   **Died** *30 B.C.*
Parents *Ptolemy XII Auletes and Cleopatra V.*
Children *Caesarion (probably by Julius Caesar) and twins (girl and boy) and son by Mark Antony.*
Personal Appearance *Probably olive complexioned with dark hair. Attractive.*
General *Extremely clever politician who spoke several languages. Combined charm with determination.*

CLEOPATRA VII (above) was the last ruler of an independent Egypt. Her cartouche (an oval with her name) is shown above.

PTOLEMY AULETES (right) was Cleopatra's father. The Ptolemies were Greek rulers of Egypt after Alexander the Great.

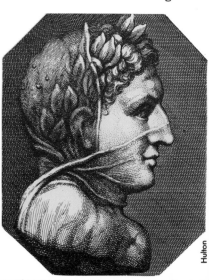

Hulton

ALEXANDRIA
ALEXANDRIA was founded by Alexander the Great in 332 B.C. and became a great commercial city and the capital of the Ptolemies. The lighthouse, one of the Seven Wonders of the World, once stood on Pharos Island in the bay. It was started by Ptolemy I, who also founded the library in Alexandria.

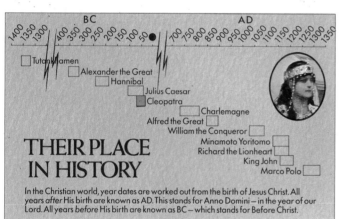

THEIR PLACE IN HISTORY

In the Christian world, year dates are worked out from the birth of Jesus Christ. All years *after* His birth are known as AD. This stands for Anno Domini – in the year of our Lord. All years *before* His birth are known as BC – which stands for Before Christ.

(Timeline: BC — Tutankhamen, Alexander the Great, Hannibal, Julius Caesar, Cleopatra; AD — Charlemagne, Alfred the Great, William the Conqueror, Minamoto Yoritomo, Richard the Lionheart, King John, Marco Polo)

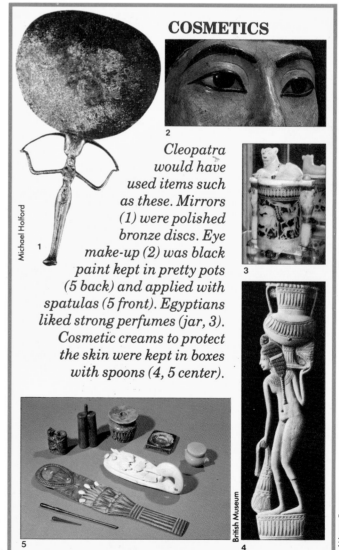

COSMETICS

Cleopatra would have used items such as these. Mirrors (1) were polished bronze discs. Eye make-up (2) was black paint kept in pretty pots (5 back) and applied with spatulas (5 front). Egyptians liked strong perfumes (jar, 3). Cosmetic creams to protect the skin were kept in boxes with spoons (4, 5 center).

her childhood, Egypt was wracked by civil war. But, at last, in 55 B.C., the Romans supporting Auletes routed the army of Cleopatra's rebellious elder sister, Berenice. The hero of the battle was a young Roman cavalry officer called Mark Antony, and it may be at this time that he and Cleopatra first met.

She was barely 15 then, a lively girl with liquid eyes and clear, olive skin. But she was extraordinarily clever and already spoke fluently in several languages. Later, it was said that hearing her voice was like listening to "an instrument of many strings."

A few years later, Auletes was dead, and Cleopatra became Pharaoh herself, in partnership with her younger brother Ptolemy XIII, as was the custom. Wisely, she took the trouble to learn Egyptian and follow Egyptian customs, and the Egyptians, especially in the south, soon came to cherish their young Greek mistress. Yet the rivalry between Cleopatra and the regents who manipulated Ptolemy had become bitter and dangerous

ANTONY AND
CLEOPATRA
Cleopatra was
accused of
captivating the two
most powerful men
in Rome to protect
her country and her
position as queen.
But Antony and
Cleopatra's love
seemed very strong.
Even after Antony's
marriage to
Octavia, he returned
and "married"
Cleopatra. He
declared her
"Queen of Kings"
and their children,
rulers.

Bridgeman

and, in 48 B.C., she had to flee the country to save her life. At that moment, Julius Caesar arrived in Alexandria and at once summoned her to him. Cleopatra was determined to go, but with Ptolemy's men all over the city, she knew she would be killed on sight if she went openly. So, one night, she set sail for Alexandria in a tiny boat, alone except for a friend named Apollodorus, and crept past Ptolemy's guards in the dark. Then, typically resourceful, she slipped inside a rolled-up carpet which Apollodorus carried into the palace. When the carpet was untied in front of Caesar, out rolled Cleopatra.

Caesar was captivated by the young Egyptian queen, and soon the two became lovers. From then on, Cleopatra's fortunes changed. In a brief but brilliant campaign, Caesar defeated Ptolemy's armies, and Ptolemy himself was killed. The two lovers celebrated their victory with a leisurely cruise up the Nile. Not long after, Cleopatra had a son (probably Caesar's) called Caesarion, and she was living in a luxurious villa in Rome. But, in his rise to

**CAESAR AND
CLEOPATRA**
Julius Caesar (right),
helped Cleopatra defeat
her brother and secure
her position as Pharaoh.
Caesar never stated that
Caesarion (left, with
Cleopatra) was his son.
But Egypt believed he
was, and Mark Antony
proclaimed Caesarion
"King of Kings."
Octavian, worried by the
threat of a new Caesar,
had Caesarion killed after
Cleopatra's death.

Spectrum

Mansell

power, Caesar had made many enemies and, in 44 B.C., he was assassinated. Cleopatra kept her misery to herself and sailed back to Egypt.

In the meantime, Mark Antony had become one of Rome's greatest generals, rivaled for power only by Caesar's nephew, Octavian. And once Caesar's assassins were beaten, the two agreed to divide the Roman world between them, with Antony taking the East and Octavian the West. Antony intended to start his reign in the East by conquering Parthia (Persia), but he needed help from Egypt. Perhaps remembering how attractive the young Cleopatra had been, he summoned her to him at Tarsus.

She stalled for a while, then came to him, and came in style. As her purple-sailed, golden boat glided up the river to Tarsus, silver oars kept time with flutes and citherns. Girls dressed as nymphs steered the helm, and the air was filled with wafts of sweet perfumes. In the center of it all, in a spectacular cloth-of-gold pavilion, lay Cleopatra herself.

Antony was intoxicated by her, and when he met Cleopatra, he fell utterly, once and for all, in love with her, and she with him. She was now at the height of her charm, not beautiful, but so captivating in manner that all who met her fell under her spell.

She and Antony spent that winter together in Alexandria in a giddy round of feasting, gaming, and hunting. But in the spring, Antony was forced to return to Rome by the death of his wife Fulvia. To patch up a quarrel with Octavian, Antony agreed to marry his rival's sister, Octavia, leaving Cleopatra alone, newly the mother of his twin son and daughter. Three years later, Antony returned to the East and Cleopatra again, and a third child was born.

In the meantime, Antony's rivalry with Octavian was building up to fever pitch, and dislike of Cleopatra did not add to Antony's popularity. In 32 B.C., the tension snapped, and the two sides began preparing for war. Antony and Cleopatra's vast fleet was soon ready. But instead of striking while Octavian was still vulnerable, Antony stopped in

CLEOPATRA'S NEEDLE

When Caesar left Egypt after his romance with Cleopatra, she had built in his honor a vast building on the sea front at Alexandria. The building was called Caesareum, and, according to legend, a pair of already ancient stone obelisks was set up in front of it. Nearly

Vivant Denon–Searight Coll/V&A

2,000 years later, when British troops landed in Egypt after defeating Napoleon, they found these two obelisks lying in the sand. The Turkish ruler of Egypt at the time made the British a present of one of them, which had originally been made for King Thutmose III in the 15th century B.C. But it was another 50 years before the obelisk, which came to be known as Cleopatra's needle, finally came to England. The needle had to be towed all the way in a specially made wooden tube, and it was almost lost in a storm in the Bay of Biscay. It was finally erected in 1867 on London's embankment, where it stands to this day. The other needle was given to America, and it can now be seen in New York City's Central Park.

Mansell

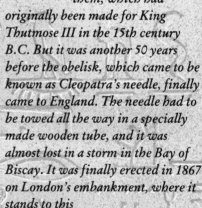

Mansell

Daily Telegraph

Oldham Picture Gallery

Oldham Picture Gallery

CLEOPATRA'S DEATH

After Antony's defeat and death, Cleopatra knew there was no future for her. She went to Octavian to beg for the lives of her children. Then, having garlanded Antony's grave, she shut herself up in her tomb with her maids Iras and Charmian and killed herself. When the Romans broke into the tomb, they found the queen and Iras dead and Charmian dying. Octavian honored Cleopatra with a splendid funeral and sent her children by Antony to Rome.

Greece. He was indecisive about invading the land (now Italy) which was his home territory. In the meantime, Octavian sailed, unmolested, across the Adriatic. Antony had missed his chance, and Antony and Cleopatra were soon trapped with their ships at Actium.

Eventually, they tried to break out, and the Battle of Actium was fought and lost. As the remnants of their fleet headed forlornly for Egypt, Antony sat with his head in his hands, speaking to no one. Back in Alexandria, Cleopatra tried to coax Antony around, but it was no good. Octavian's progress toward them was swift and relentless. Cleopatra retreated to her tomb.

Afraid of Antony's temper, Cleopatra barred herself in and sent word that she was dead. In his grief, Antony fell upon his sword. Then, fatally wounded, he was carried to Cleopatra's tomb. When she saw her dying lover, Cleopatra cried out in anguish and struggled to haul his body up into the tomb. Antony died in her arms.

Octavian posted guards to stop Cleopatra from escaping. But she was too clever for him, and had a deadly snake—the asp—brought into her in a basket of figs. The snake gave its fatal bite, and the most famous of Egypt's queens passed away into history.

Roger Viollet

ISIS

Cleopatra closely associated herself with the goddess Isis, who married her own brother Osiris. Like the gods, Pharaohs usually married and ruled with their sisters or brothers. Egyptians liked for their Pharaohs to have a link with the gods, and Cleopatra especially stressed Isis' maternal appeal. She also attended the holy ceremony of the Apis Bull in 51 B.C., where she was hailed as Pharaoh.

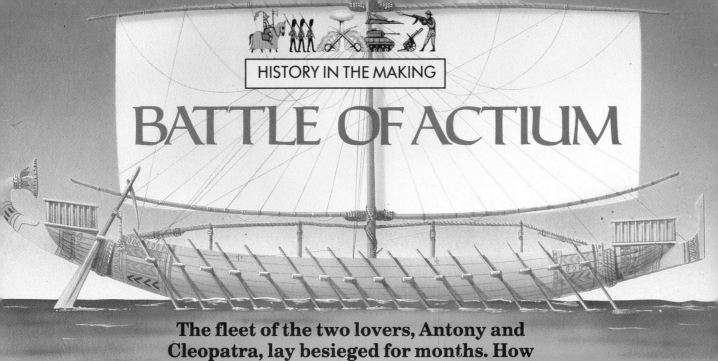

BATTLE OF ACTIUM

The fleet of the two lovers, Antony and Cleopatra, lay besieged for months. How could they defeat Octavian?

September 2, 31 B.C. The Roman Consul Octavian paced impatiently around the deck of his war galley. Already sweating a little in his heavy battle armor, he paused a while and leaned against the warm wooden deck rail. His great battle fleet stretched away over the sea. Altogether, Octavian had perhaps 250 galleys that day. His opponent, Mark Antony, he reckoned, could count on about 200 war galleys, most of them heavier than his.

There were 40,000 of the best soldiers from Rome crowded on the decks and fighting towers of Octavian's ships. Down below in the gloom sat row upon row of half-naked oarsmen, each trying to guess what was going on above.

Far away to his left, at the northern end of the line, Octavian glimpsed the galley of Marcus Vipsanius Agrippa and thanked the gods he had such a fine commander on his side. It was Agrippa who had captured the island of Leucas to the southwest of Actium, which meant he could cut off the ships bringing grain to Antony's army.

In front, Octavian could see the parched

Mauro Pucciarelli

CLEOPATRA

Mauro Pucciarelli

MARK ANTONY

Scala

OCTAVIAN

FESTIVITIES
On the way to Actium, Cleopatra and Antony stopped at the isle of Samos. Here, the most spectacular feasts and entertainments took place. Then they sailed to Athens, where they enjoyed more feasting. But Octavian was busy preparing for war, and Antony's delay was a fatal error.

49

MARK ANTONY LEAVING THE BATTLE

Stephen Biesty

peninsula of Actium, guarding the entrance to the Gulf of Ambracia where Antony's fleet had been bottled up for so many months.

But where was Antony? Surely his fleet should have made a move by now? Time was on Octavian's side, it was true, for Antony's food supplies were dwindling rapidly, and more deserters were coming across to Octavian every day. Antony had tried to cut off their water supplies, but had failed. Octavian's army had already been at Actium for four months, and morale was low.

Then at last, about nine in the morning, Antony's great fleet came gliding smoothly over the bar that marked the entrance to the

Gulf and fanned out into the bay between Parginosuala Point and Cape Scylla. Bringing up the rear came Cleopatra herself, her ships as splendid as ever in the morning sun.

Yet, instead of coming on toward Octavian's fleet, Antony's ships came to a stop inside the bay and lay silently on their oars. Why? Was Antony trying to draw Octavian's fleet into the bay? If so, Agrippa didn't take up the challenge and for more than two hours, the two great fleets sat motionless in the sunshine, facing each other across the calm sea. Then, about noon, Antony's fleet began to edge forward, first the left wing to the south, and then the right, with Antony's flag ship.

At once, Octavian's fleet started to back away, hoping to draw the Antonians far out into open water. But after little more than half a mile, they stopped backing and stood their ground.

Within minutes, Antony's fleet was closing in on them. As they came nearer, a stream of missiles came flying from catapults perched on the decks. Soldiers ducked as rocks, nails, and firebombs came whistling toward them. Most splashed harmlessly in the sea, but many hit their mark, scattering men and splintering the deck. Then came a hail of arrows from men in the towers.

At last, with a terrible thump, crunch, and creak, the two fleets met. The sea churned and foamed as the galleys clashed. Oars snapped. Timber groaned. Men cried out in anger and pain, and the air between the ships was filled with a barrage of spears and missiles.

Within minutes, many of the ships had drawn along-

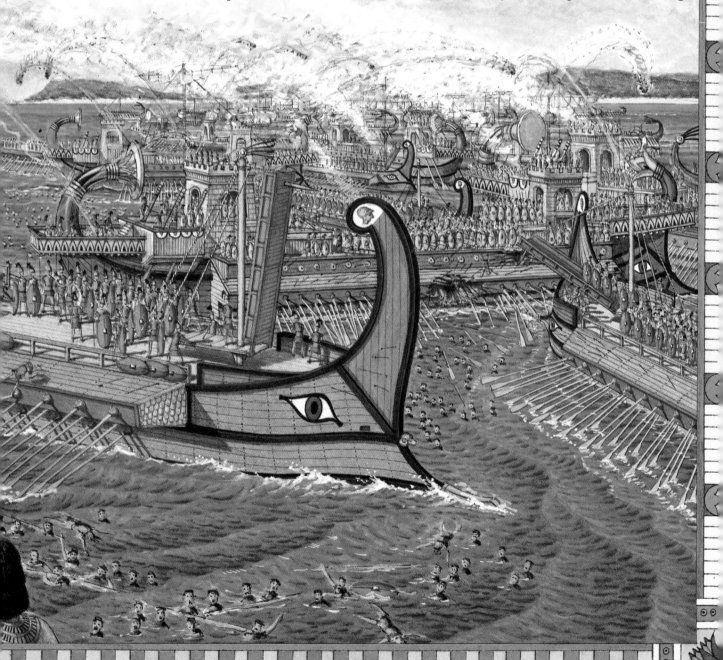

Scala

side and grappling irons were flung across to yank them together. Then, the *corvus*, or bridge, was let down onto the decks. Soon, men were swarming from one ship to another, and fearsome hand-to-hand fighting began. Arrows continued to rain down from above, and decks and sea alike were soon stained with blood.

From the start, Agrippa had tried to outflank Antony at the north. Antony countered by extending his right wing northward, and a gap began to appear in the center, where he had placed his less experienced captains. The center soon became the scene of a desperate struggle—which may be what Antony had intended.

Suddenly, at the height of the battle—about 2:30 in the afternoon—something happened which left Octavian's men gasping in amazement. As they watched, Cleopatra's squadron hoisted its sails and sailed swiftly away on the afternoon breeze, gliding clear out from the midst of the fighting. Soon, her ships were rounding the island of Leucas and streaming away to the south.

At this time, Antony's ship was caught inextricably in a fierce melée. But when he saw Cleopatra heading away, he leaped onto another ship and sailed off after her.

After that, it was soon over. Some of Antony's ships managed to escape from the tangle and follow their leader. But the rest were stuck. They fought on for another hour or so and then started to surrender. By dusk, the sea was quiet.

Ever since the Battle of Actium, people have tried to explain the events of that day, especially Cleopatra's flight from the battle. Romans, who made Octavian the hero of the battle, made Cleopatra the villain—an Egyptian temptress who was such a coward that she deserted her noble, but misguided, lover Antony when the going got rough. And Antony was so totally besotted by her that he abandoned his fleet and his honor to go after her.

WAR GALLEY
(left) This carving may commemorate the Battle of Actium—certainly galleys like these were part of Octavian's fleet.

ROMAN COIN
(below) struck to celebrate the defeat of Antony and Cleopatra. It is inscribed with the Egyptian crocodile and the words "Egypt Captured."

Werner Forman

But there is another way of looking at the events. With a smaller fleet and morale low because of the blockade, Antony must have known that he had little chance of beating Octavian. He could not stay in Actium much longer; the situation was desperate. That day, then, could he have been trying to escape with as much of his fleet as possible?

Antony may have been waiting until midday for the wind that often springs up along the Adriatic coast to help make a quick getaway to the south. That morning, Antony had sails stowed on his ships, which was unusual when going into battle, since sails were heavy. He told his men the sails were for pursuing the beaten enemy, but perhaps this was just to stop them from worrying. If so, then Cleopatra was not deserting, but leaving first according to plan, through the gap in the center of the battle deliberately opened up by Antony.

We shall probably never know the truth. The Battle of Actium was the end for both Antony and Cleopatra and the turning point in Octavian's progress toward complete power over the Roman world.

MEDALLION of the Battle of Actium was engraved in 1740.

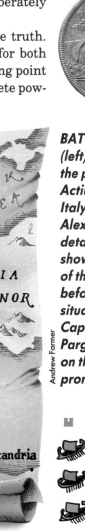

Peter Clayton

BATTLE PLAN
(left) This map shows the position of Actium in relation to Italy and Alexandria. The detailed picture shows the positions of the fleets just before the battle, situated between Cape Scylla and Parginosuala Point on the opposite promontory.

Susan Moxley

Andrew Farmer

🏰 Fort

🚢 Antony's Fleet

🚢 Agrippa's Fleet

🚢 Cleopatra's Fleet

A SCRIBE'S STORY

As the sun beats down on the quayside at ancient Alexandria, a scribe takes time to describe what he is doing

There is a text of ancient wisdom in the temple which says, "Behold, there is no calling that is without a master but that of a scribe, and he is the master." Well, I am a scribe, and maybe I'm my own man, too, but writing is sometimes hard work, I can tell you.

Just now, as I sit in the sun on the quay at Alexandria, I am writing furiously with this reed brush on papyrus [paper made from papyrus reeds]. Every now and then, I

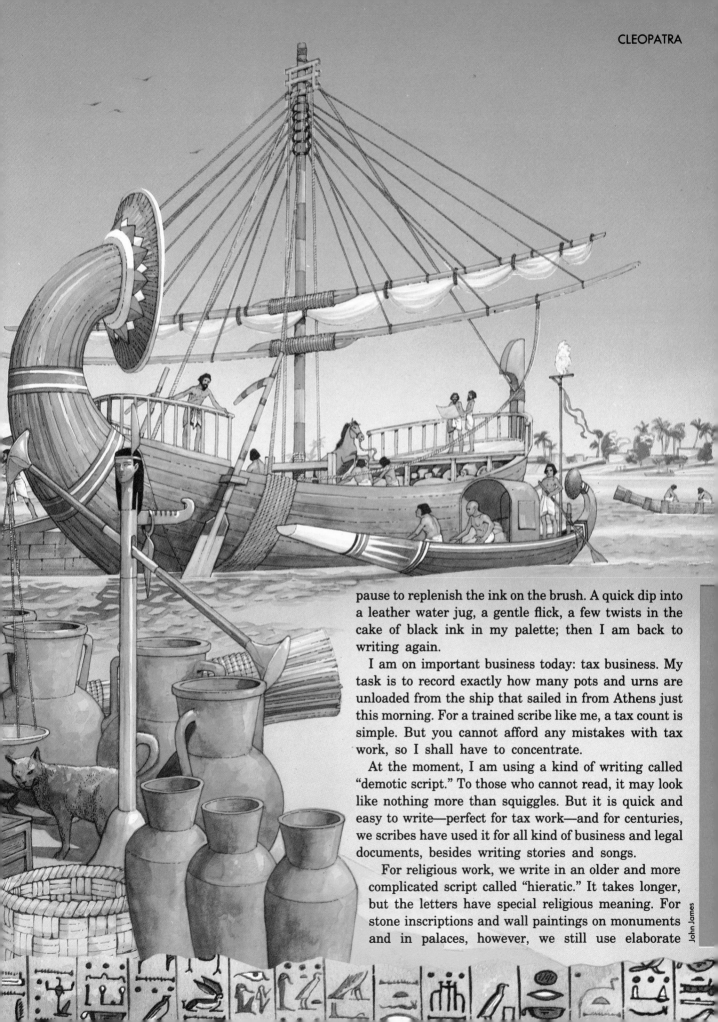

pause to replenish the ink on the brush. A quick dip into a leather water jug, a gentle flick, a few twists in the cake of black ink in my palette; then I am back to writing again.

I am on important business today: tax business. My task is to record exactly how many pots and urns are unloaded from the ship that sailed in from Athens just this morning. For a trained scribe like me, a tax count is simple. But you cannot afford any mistakes with tax work, so I shall have to concentrate.

At the moment, I am using a kind of writing called "demotic script." To those who cannot read, it may look like nothing more than squiggles. But it is quick and easy to write—perfect for tax work—and for centuries, we scribes have used it for all kind of business and legal documents, besides writing stories and songs.

For religious work, we write in an older and more complicated script called "hieratic." It takes longer, but the letters have special religious meaning. For stone inscriptions and wall paintings on monuments and in palaces, however, we still use elaborate

John James

ancient picture letters called "hieroglyphs," which date back thousands of years to around 3000 B.C. There are over 700 of these hieroglyphs, and they can only be drawn slowly, but they are sacred and we believe the images possess unique powers.

Hieroglyphs are very old, it is true. But I believe there are even older forms of writing. It is said that the Sumerians in the kingdom of Mesopotamia [now Syria] were the first to create a proper written language, slightly earlier than us. The Sumerians used different wedge-shaped marks [cuneiforms] made on clay tablets to represent different sounds—so they could write down words as they were spoken.

By Thoth! I almost missed that one. Counting pots really does need all your attention! I'm not at all sure I'm cut out for this. I should explain that it was Thoth who we believe gave us writing. He is the patron god of scribes, and his symbol is always the palette, brush, and jug of the scribe.

Scribes are needed for many other things in Egypt besides tax work. The army needs scribes to keep a track of supplies and to advise when new recruits are needed. The temples need scribes to help them run efficiently and co-ordinate the housing and feeding of thousands of priests. And scribes are needed at Cleopatra's palace in Alexandria, too, to record laws and to communicate her wishes, but because we are now ruled by Greeks, the court uses the Greek language which most of us Egyptians do not understand.

My father always wanted me to be a scribe because Egyptians respect a scribe's learning. When I was young, he would say, "Son, I have seen the smith at his work beside his furnace. His fingers are like crocodile skin, and he stinks worse than fish roe. The washerman spends his whole day going up and down, and he is always weak through whitening his neighbors' clothes. As for the farmer, he croaks like a crow; and if he ever rests, he lies down in the mud. So be a scribe, son; it is the profession of a prince."

So, at the age of five, off I went to school at the temple to learn to read, write, and do arithmetic. Only the rich could go to these schools, for you had to pay the priests well, so I was lucky, I suppose. But I was at the school for 12 years, and hated every minute.

It was always such hard work, and the teachers were so cruel. "A boy's ears are in his back," one teacher would say. "He listens when you beat him." Every day, I remember praying for noon to come quickly, for then my mother would come, bringing three rolls of bread and two jugs of barley wine.

FLASH BACK

The Egyptians worshiped many gods. They had shrines in their homes—a statue in a corner—and built temples where priests carried out rituals. This temple (above) was built at Kalabsha to worship Horus and Isis.

The temple of Philae (below) is dedicated to Isis, the mother goddess. The temple had to be moved stone by stone to a new site to keep it from being submerged when the Egyptians built the Aswan dam across the Nile in the 1970s.

TEMPLES of the PTOLEMIES

The beautiful temple at Dendera (right), begun by Ptolemy IX, was added to by his successors, including Cleopatra. It was for Hathor, goddess of creation and joy. The tops of the pillars are carved with a likeness of her face.

Bridgeman

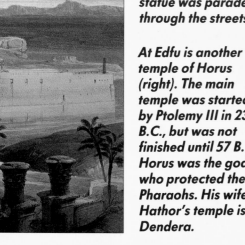

Sonia Halliday

Giraudon

In ancient times, Dendera was an important town, but today the temple (above) stands in isolation. On special days, Hathor's statue was paraded through the streets.

The ruins of the temple of Kom Ombo (left). It was built for the worship of Sobek, the crocodile-headed god, and Horus, who had the head of a falcon. The temple was divided so each god had half, and there were two front doors.

At Edfu is another temple of Horus (right). The main temple was started by Ptolemy III in 237 B.C., but was not finished until 57 B.C. Horus was the god who protected the Pharaohs. His wife Hathor's temple is at Dendera.

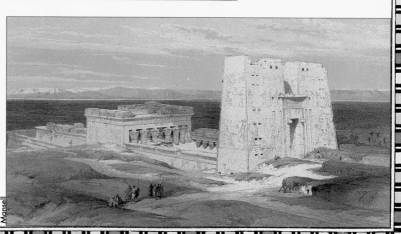

Mansell

SHIPS OF THE NILE

Michael Holford

The dhow (left) and the felucca (below) are cargo boats commonly found on the Nile today.

J Allan Cash

This wall painting (below) from a tomb in Thebes shows an ancient Egyptian boat made from planks pegged and lashed together.

A model boat (above) left in a tomb for travel in the afterlife. Boats sailed upstream, but were rowed downstream.

Ronald Sheridan

Gold pendant (above) of a ship with a duck-headed stern. An Egyptian craft (right) made of bundles of papyrus lashed together.

Mansell

From the earliest times, the Egyptians have used the Nile as a means of moving animals and goods up and down their country, as they still do today.

Like the mountains, lessons seemed to endure forever, for we had much to learn. All day long, from dawn to dusk, we copied out ancient texts to help us learn these scripts. We were never allowed to use papyrus, for it is expensive. Instead, we wrote on flakes of pottery or stone, or sometimes wood. It was all boring, repetitive work. Only in our last few years at school did we start to learn how to write letters and do bookkeeping and arithmetic.

Now I can see that was all worthwhile. If I do well at my job, I can, as a scribe, rise to the highest ranks in the country. Like Amenhotep-Son-of-Hapu more than a thousand years ago, I could become head of public works, chief tax collector, or even chief architect. And like Amenhotep, too, I might one day be granted a permit by the Pharaoh to build a funeral temple of my own.

If I can do that, then I shall indeed have done well. I will have earned for myself a high place in the next world as well as this.

GLOSSARY

absolute Total and complete.

arduous Requiring great toil and effort.

arena Area, usually oval, in a Roman amphitheatre, in which contests took place.

barbarian A wild and uncouth person lacking learning or culture.

besotted Infatuated, having all faculties dulled by love.

cat nap Brief, light sleep.

centurion Commander in the Roman army, in charge of a century (originally a company of 100 soldiers).

cithern Musical instrument strung with wires.

commercial Concerning buying and selling.

classical Term used to describe the art of ancient Greece and Rome, especially its qualities of order and harmony.

Consul One of the two chief magistrates of ancient Rome, elected for one year.

crescent The shape of the moon in the first or last quarter when less than half is visible.

decoy Someone or something used to divert attention from an enemy's intended target and to lead that enemy into a trap.

Dictator Person granted absolute power over the government of Rome.

drill Training in military exercises.

Epicureanism School of philosophy founded by Epicurus, a Greek philosopher, in the fourth century B.C. Emphasis was placed on the identification of good with pleasure – "we declare pleasure to be the beginning and end of the blessed life" – and the cultivation of emotional calm, intellectual pleasures and friendship.

esparto grass Type of grass used to make paper, cord, and rope.

fervent Intense.

fluent Speaking quickly and effortlessly, particularly in a foreign language.

fodder Animal food, usually dried.

forum Market place in a Roman city where public business took place.

Gaul Territory that included modern-day France, Belgium, western Germany and northern Italy.

Hulton

gorge A narrow passage through steep-walled land.

gladiator Person trained to fight with a sword or other weapon for public entertainment in ancient Rome – usually a fight to the death.

grappling iron A hooked iron with rope attached, used to fasten an enemy ship alongside before boarding.

guile Cunning.

hieroglyphs Ancient system of writing using pictorial characters to depict sounds or words.

Jupiter King of the gods in Roman mythology. Known as Zeus in ancient Greece.

mattock Ancient agricultural tool used for digging.

mausoleum Elaborate tomb in which the dead are buried, usually above ground.

melée Confused skirmish or struggle.

mirage Optical illusion caused by hot air near the surface of the earth.

missile Object thrown through the air to cause injury or damage to someone or something at a distance.

molest To attack with intention to injure.

morale Moral condition of confidence, enthusiasm and well-being.

obelisk Large, upright, four-sided pillar which tapers toward the top to end in a pyramid shape.

offerings Gifts ceremonially given as part of worship.

palette Thin board used for holding and mixing painting or writing materials.

peninsula Piece of land surrounded on three sides by water.

Patrician A member of one of the original, privileged, citizen families in ancient Rome.

Plebeian A member of the common people in ancient Rome (as opposed to the privileged **Patrician** class).

ponderous Heavy, unwieldy, and slow-moving.

Praetorian Guard The personal guard of the Roman Emperor.

pyre Bonfire lit at funerals for the burning of the corpse.

retaliation Repayment of insult or injury in kind; getting even.

ritual Ceremony performed as an act of worship.

rostra (Latin) Roman platform for public speeches.

script System of handwriting.

Senate The supreme council and chief governing body of ancient Rome.

shrine Area devoted to worship.

sinew Fibrous tissue connecting muscle to bone.

sporadic Occurring at odd intervals, intermittent, not continuous.

stampede Panicked, directionless rush of frightened animals.

Stoicism School of philosophy founded by Zeno in Athens, Greece, in 308 B.C. Emphasis was placed on reason and virtue.

strigil Instrument used for scraping the skin after bathing or exercise.

terracotta (Italian) Reddish brown clay, baked and usually unglazed, used for tiles and pottery. (Terracotta is Italian for "cooked earth.")

Tribune A Roman official elected to protect the rights of the common people (**Plebeians**) and to defend them against unfair legislation proposed by **Patricians**.

triumvirate Ruling group of three people.

vassal Slave; humble dependant.

veto The power to forbid the enactment of laws.

whiff The slightest trace or hint.

CHRONOLOGY

The Roman World 270 B.C. to A.D. 30

Note In the Christian world, year dates are worked out from the birth of Jesus Christ. All years after His birth are known as A.D. This stands for Anno Domini (in the year of our Lord). All years before His birth are known as B.C., which stands for Before Christ.

	POLITICS AND WAR	RELIGION AND LEARNING
270 B.C. to 210 B.C.	**264-241 B.C.** First Punic War between Rome and powerful rival, Carthage. **247 B.C.** Hannibal, Carthaginian general, born. **238 B.C.** Carthage begins the conquest of Spain. **222 B.C.** Northern Italy conquered by Rome. **219-202 B.C.** Second Punic War. Carthaginians under Hannibal invade Italy. Finally forced to leave by Roman general Scipio. **215-205 B.C.** First Macedonian War between Rome and Macedon (in Greece).	**c.250 B.C.** Arcesilaus, Greek philosopher, founds a second Academy in Athens. **237 B.C.** The temple of the sun god Horus is begun at Edfu, Egypt. **c.225 B.C.** Quintus Fabius Pictor, the first Roman historian, born. Although his great work, a history of Rome from the earliest times, is now lost, it was used as a source by later Roman historians such as Livy.
209 B.C. to 150 B.C.	**200-197 B.C.** Second Macedonian War between Rome and Macedon. **192 B.C.** Rome defeats the Greek city state of Sparta. **183 B.C.** Scipio dies. **183 B.C.** Pisa and Parma in Italy become colonies of Rome. **183 B.C.** While in exile, Hannibal kills himself to avoid capture by Rome. **171-163 B.C.** Third Macedonian War. Macedon submits to Roman rule and is given a Roman governor.	**c.200 B.C.** Inscription engraved on the Rosetta stone. After its discovery in 1799, the stone's text, written in Egyptian and Greek, enabled Egyptian hieroglyphic writing to be translated. **168 B.C.** Antiochus IV of Syria sets up an altar to the Greek god Zeus in the temple at Jerusalem. Leads to a Jewish revolt under Judas Maccabeus. **c.165 B.C.** Old Testament *Book of Daniel* written. **164 B.C.** Judas Maccabeus reconsecrates the Temple after expelling the Syrians.
149 B.C. to 90 B.C.	**149-146 B.C.** Third Punic War. Carthage is defeated and the city is destroyed. **147 B.C.** Greece comes under Roman control. **133 B.C.** Asia Minor becomes a Roman province. **100 B.C.** Julius Caesar born. **91-89 B.C.** War between Rome and other Italian cities. Rome is victorious and grants other Italians Roman citizenship.	**c.110 B.C.** Pharisees and Sadducees become important in Palestine. **c.100 B.C.** Great Stupa (Buddhist shrine) built at Sanchi, India. **c.94 B.C.** Roman poet and philosopher, Lucretius, born. **90 B.C.** Vitruvius writes his book, *On Architecture,* a guide for Roman architects. This work has remained one of the most important source books for classical architecture.
89 B.C. to 30 B.C.	**73-71 B.C.** Roman slaves rebel, led by Spartacus. Defeated by Consuls, Pompey and Crassus. **63 B.C.** Pompey conquers Jerusalem. **63 B.C.** Octavian (future emperor Augustus) born. **58-50 B.C.** Caesar conquers Gaul. **55 B.C.** Caesar invades Britain. **49-45 B.C.** Civil war between Caesar and Pompey. Caesar wins and becomes Dictator. **44 B.C.** Caesar assassinated. Civil war begins. **42 B.C.** Battle of Philippi. Brutus and Cassius, leaders of Caesar's murderers, defeated by Antony and Octavian. **31 B.C.** Battle of Actium. Mark Antony and Cleopatra defeated by Octavian. **30 B.C.** Octavian, renamed Augustus, becomes virtual Emperor of Rome.	**60 B.C.** Lucretius writes his poem, *On the Nature of Things,* a description of the theories of the Greek philosopher Epicurus. **55 B.C.** Cicero, Roman statesman, lawyer, and writer, writes his book, *On the Republic.* **51 B.C.** Caesar writes his *Commentaries on the Gallic War,* his account of his conquests. **47 B.C.** Library at Alexandria, the most famous library of the ancient world, partly destroyed during Caesar's siege of the city.
29 B.C. to A.D.30	**9 B.C.** Roman army under Drusus and Tiberius reaches the Elbe river in Germany. **A.D. 6** Judea becomes a Roman province. **A.D. 14** Augustus dies and is succeeded by Tiberius. **A.D. 26** Tiberius retires to the island of Capri, leaving Sejanus (head of the Praetorian Guard) to govern Rome.	**4 B.C.** Lucius Annaeus Seneca, Roman philosopher, statesman and dramatist, born. **c.4 B.C.** Jesus Christ born at Bethlehem. **A.D. 17** Roman historian Livy dies. His most famous work was a history of Rome from the foundation of the city to the reign of the Emperor Augustus. **A.D. 30** Probable date of Christ's crucifixion in Jerusalem.

In 270 B.C., Rome was a minor Italian state. During the next 250 years, she expanded around the Mediterranean Sea until she controlled much of the then known world.

During these years of conquest, Rome was a republic, but Octavian's victories transformed the city into an imperial capital with himself – renamed Augustus – as emperor.

ART AND LITERATURE	SCIENCE AND SOCIETY	
250 B.C. Plautus, Roman comic playwright, born. His works, which were adapted from Greek originals, created a truly Latin drama. **239 B.C.** Ennius, Roman poet, born. He was one of the most important early poets to use the Latin language and has been called the founder of Roman literature. **225 B.C.** The Colossus of Rhodes (a 100-feet-high bronze statue at the mouth of Rhodes harbor) destroyed by an earthquake.	**268 B.C.** First mention of the Roman silver coin, the denarius. **264 B.C.** First recorded public combat between gladiators takes place in Rome. **228 B.C.** New Carthage (Cartagena) founded in Spain by Hasdrubal. **215 B.C.** Great Wall of China built to keep out Western invaders. **212 B.C.** Greek mathematician Archimedes killed during the Roman capture of Sicily.	**270 B.C. to 210 B.C.**
c.200 B.C. Gnaeus Naevius, Roman comedy writer and poet, born. He was one of the first to write plays based on Rome's history. **191 B.C.** Plautus writes his comic play, *Pseudolus*. **c.185 B.C.** Terence, Roman playwright, born. His plays are the basis of the modern "comedy of manners." **167 B.C.** Terence's play, *Andria*, performed in Rome.	**200 B.C.** Cato the Elder writes his book on agriculture. **180 B.C.** The first stone bridge (the Aemilian Bridge) built in Rome. **c.170 B.C.** Paved streets are first made in Rome. **c.160 B.C.** A water-driven clock is erected in Rome.	**209 B.C. to 150 B.C.**
c.140 B.C. The *Venus of Milo* statue is sculpted. Now in the Louvre Museum, Paris. **c.118 B.C.** Polybius, Greek historian and statesman, dies. His most famous work was a history of the Punic wars between Rome and Carthage. **c.103 B.C.** Lucilius, satirical author, dies. **c.100 B.C.** Cornelius Nepos, Roman historian and a friend of Cicero, born.	**c.105 B.C.** Heron, Greek mathematician, founds a College of Technology in Alexandria, Egypt. **100 B.C.** Ships of China reach the east coast of India. **90 B.C.** Asclepiades, a Greek doctor famous in the ancient world, practices medicine in Rome.	**149 B.C. to 90 B.C.**
87 B.C. Roman poet Catullus born. He is best known for his poems to the faithless Lesbia. **86 B.C.** Sallust, Roman historian, born. His most famous work deals with the Catiline conspiracy. **70 B.C.** Virgil, Roman poet, born. His epic poem, the *Aeneid*, describes the founding of Rome by the mythical Trojan, Aeneas. **43 B.C.** Ovid, Roman poet, born. **c.40 B.C.** The *Laocoon* is sculpted. When it was rediscovered, this marble statue inspired Michelangelo. **30 B.C.** Work begins on the Pantheon in Rome.	**63 B.C.** A system of shorthand is invented by Marcus Tullius Tiro, one of Cicero's slaves. **62 B.C.** The city of Florence is founded in Italy. **54 B.C.** Work begins, under the direction of Julius Caesar, on the Julian forum in Rome. **46 B.C.** Caesar introduces the Julian calendar of 365¼ days. The calendar also included a leap year and was used in the United States and Great Britain until the 1750s.	**89 B.C. to 30 B.C.**
4 B.C. Seneca, Roman playwright and statesman, born. Became very influential in government during the reign of the notorious Emperor Nero. **1 B.C.** Ovid's poem, *Ars Amatoria* (The Art of Love), published. **A.D. 5** Ovid writes the *Metamorphoses,* a long poem describing a series of mythological metamorphoses (changes). **A.D. 8** Ovid banished by the Emperor Augustus on charges of immorality.	**7 B.C.** Augustus divides Romes into *regiones* (wards) and *vici* (precincts). **A.D. 6** Augustus organizes a professional fire department for the city of Rome. **A.D. 23** Pliny born. His most famous work was the *Natural History*, a scientific encyclopedia. Pliny died during the eruption of the volcano Vesuvius. **A.D. 25** Strabo, author of the *Geographia*, dies. His work drew together knowledge of world geography from many ancient writers.	**29 B.C. to A.D. 30**

FURTHER READING

Peter Bull

Bains, Rae, *Ancient Greece.* Troll Associates (Mahwah, 1985)

Brandt, Keith, *Ancient Rome.* Troll Associates (Mahwah, 1985)

Bruns, Roger, *Julius Caesar.* Chelsea House (Edgemont, 1987)

Chijioke, F. A., *Ancient Africa.* Holmes & Meier (New York, 1969)

Connolly, Peter, *Hannibal and the Enemies of Rome.* Silver, Burdett & Ginn (Lexington, 1985)

Corbishley, Mike, *The Roman World.* Watts, Franklin (New York, 1986)

Forman, Joan, *The Romans.* Silver, Burdett & Ginn (Lexington, 1985)

Hirsh, Marilyn, *Hannibal and His Thirty-Seven Elephants.* Holiday House (New York, 1977)

Hoobler, Dorothy and Thomas, *Cleopatra.* Chelsea House (Edgemont, 1986)

Hughes, Jill, *Imperial Rome.* Watts, Franklin (New York, 1985)

Kittredge, Mary, *Mark Antony.* Chelsea House (Edgemont, 1988)

May, Robin, *Julius Caesar and the Romans.* Watts, Franklin (New York, 1984)

Miquel, Pierre, *Ancient Egyptians.* Silver, Burdett & Ginn (Lexington, 1985)

Payne, Elizabeth, *The Pharaohs of Ancient Egypt.* Random House (New York, 1981)

Rutland, Jonathan, *See Inside a Roman Town.* Watts, Franklin (New York, 1986)

Santrey, Laurence, *Ancient Egypt.* Troll Associates (Mahwah, 1985)

Shakespeare, William, *Julius Caesar* (adapted by Diana Stewart). Raintree Publications (Milwaukee, 1983)

Usher, Kerry, *Heroes, Gods and Emperors from Roman Mythology.* Schocken Books (New York, 1984)

Weigall, Arthur E., *Life and Times of Cleopatra, Queen of Egypt.* Greenwood Press (Westport, 1968)

Wells, Reuben, F., *On Land and Sea with Caesar.* Biblo & Tannen (Cheshire, 1926)

Wells, Reuben F., *With Caesar's Legions.* Biblo & Tannen (Cheshire, 1951)

Wilkes, John, *The Roman Army.* Lerner Publications (Minneapolis, 1977)

INDEX

Bridgeman

NOTE Page numbers in italic type refer to illustrations.

AB

Actium, Battle of 48, 49-53, *49-53*
Agrippa, Marcus Vipsanius 49, 51, 52
Alesia, Siege of *34-35*, 36, 37
Alexander the Great *30*, 44, *44*, 45
Alexandria 44, *45*, *46*, *47*, *53*, 54, *54-55*, 56
Alps 15, 17, *17*, 20, *20*
Antony, Mark 44, 45, *46*, 47, 48, *48*, 49, *49*, 50, *50*, 51, 52, 53, *53*
Apollodorus 46
Augustus *32*
  see also Octavian
Auletes *32*
Aurelia 28
Baal 24, *24*, 25-26
baths, Roman 41, *41*, 42
Britain 34, 47, *47*

C

Caesar, Caius Julius (father of Julius Caesar) 28

Caesar, Julius 28, *31*, 39, 44, *46*
  as Curule Aedile 29, 30
  birth 28
  bribing of voters 30
  capture by pirates *29*
  childhood 28
  Cicero and 30
  crossing the Rubicon 31, *31*
  death 28, 32, *32*, 47
  envy of Alexander the Great *30*
  first meeting with Cleopatra 46
  governance of Rome 32
  image on coin *32*
  marriage 28
  personal profile 28
  raid on Britain 31
  refusal of crown, 28, *29*, 32
  selection as Consul 30
  study of public speaking 29
  triumphs/triumphal processions 32, 33-37, *33-37*
  "Veni, Vidi, Vici" speech 32
  views on Catilina 30
Caesarion 28, 46, *46*
Calpurnia 28, *31*

Cannae, Battle of 15, *15*
Cartagena 13, *13*
Carthage 12, *12*, 13, *13*, *14*, *15*, 16, *16*, 18, 20, 22-26, *22-26*
Catilina, Lucius Sergius 30
Cato 16
Charmian 48
Cicero, Marcus Tullius 30, *30*
Cleopatra VII 31, *44*, *46*, *49*, 56, 57
  as Pharaoh 45, *48*
  Battle of Actium and 51, 52, 53, *53*
  birth 44
  cartouche *44*
  childhood 45
  death 44, *46*, 48, *48*
  first meeting with Julius Caesar 46
  Mark Antony and 45, *46*, 47, 48
  personal profile 44
  tomb 44
Cleopatra V (mother of Cleopatra VII) 44
Cleopatra's Needle, London 47, *47*
Cornelia 28
cosmetics, Egyptian *45*
Crassus, Marcus Licinius 29-30, 31

DEF

Dido, Queen of Carthage 12, 23
Egypt/Egyptians 23, 24, 31, 44, *44*, 45, *46*, 47, 48, *48*, 52, *53*, 56, *56*, 58
elephants *14*, 15, 17, *17*, 18, *18-19*, 20, 21, 25
Fabius *15*
forum, Roman 28, *29*, *39*
Fulvia 47

GH

games, Roman 42, *42*
Gaul/Gauls 17, 19, 30, 31, 32, 33, *33*, 34, *34-35*, 36, 37
Greece/Greeks 24, 25, 28, *29*, 31, *44*, 45, 47, 48, 56
Hamilcar Barca 12, *12*, *13*, 22
Hannibal *12*, 22, 23, 40
  as magistrate 16
  Battle of Cannae and 15
  birth 12
  campaign against corruption 16
  crossing the Alps 15, 17-21, *17-21*
  death by poison 12, 16, *16*
  defeat by Scipio *14*, 16, 26
  defense of Carthage 16
  election as supreme military leader in Spain 13
  exile 16
  Fabius and *15*
  fear of assassination 14
  forces *21*
  image on coin *16*
  marriage 14
  meaning of name 26
  military training 13
  oath against Rome 13, *13*

personal characteristics 13-14
personal profile 12
shield *16*
Hanno 25
Hasdrubal the Splendid 13, 14, 26
Hathor 57
hieroglyphs 56
Horus 56, 57, *57*

IJ

Iarbus 23
Ides of March 32, *32*
Imilce 14
Iras 44, *48*
Isis *48*, 56
Italy 17, 20, 21, 31, 47, *53*
Juba, King of Numidia 32
Julia 28
Jupiter 28, 39

LM

Lupercalian Festival 28, 32
Mago 25
Mediterranean Sea 12, 22, 25, 34, 37
Mithridates 32
Molon, Apollonius 29, *29*

NOP

Nile River 31, 46, *56*, 58, *58*
Octavia 47
Octavian *32*, 44, *46*, 47, 48, *48*, 49, *49*, 50, 51, 52, 53, *53*
  see also Augustus
Osiris *48*
papyrus 54, 58, *58*
Pharnaces 32
Phoenicians 12, 23, 24, 25

Pompeia 28
Pompeius, Gnaeus (Pompey) 30, 31
Ptolemy I *45*
Ptolemy III 57
Ptolemy IX 57
Ptolemy XII Auletes 44, *44*
Ptolemy XIII 31, 45, 46, *46*, *48*
Punic Wars 12, 14, 22, 26

RS

Remus 38
Rhine River *37*
Rhodes 29, *29*
Rhône River 17, *17*
Rome/Romans 12, 13, 14, *14*, 15, 16, *16*, 20, 22, 23, 24, 25, *25*, 26, 28, 29, *29*, 30, 31, 32, *32*, *33*, 37, 38-42, *38-42*, 44, 45, 46, *46*, 47, *48*, 49, 52, 53
Romulus 38, 39
Rubicon River 31, *31*
Scipio (Africanus) *14*, 16, 26
Senate, Roman 30, *30*, 32, *32*
Spain 12, *12*, 13, *13*, 14, *14*, 17, 23, 32, 33, *33*

T

Tanit 24, *24*, 26
Tarquinus Superbus 40
Thutmose III 47
Tiber River 38
Tunisia 12

VZ

Varro 15
Vercingetorix *33*, 34, 36, 37
Zama, Battle of *14*, 16